PUB WALKS *for* MOTORISTS

Kent, Surrey and Sussex

MICHAEL EASTERBROOK
AND
DAVID WELLER

COUNTRYSIDE BOOKS
NEWBURY BERKSHIRE

First published 2003
© Michael Easterbrook 2003
© David Weller 2003

COUNTRYSIDE BOOKS
3 Catherine Road
Newbury, Berkshire

To view our complete range of books,
please visit us at
www.countrysidebooks.co.uk

ISBN 1 85306 797 0

Photographs by the authors
Cover photographs by David Sellman and Derek Forss
Cover design by Peter Davies, Nautilus Design

Produced through MRM Associates Ltd., Reading
Printed by Woolnough Bookbinding Ltd., Irthlingborough

Contents

INTRODUCTION

WALKS IN KENT

1. **Fordcombe:** The Chafford Arms (5 miles) — 9
2. **Eynsford:** The Plough (5½ miles) — 12
3. **Ightham:** The George and Dragon (6 miles) — 15
4. **West Malling:** The Five-pointed Star (4 miles) — 18
5. **Brenchley:** The Bull (4 miles) — 21
6. **Sissinghurst:** The Bull (4¼ or 7 miles) — 24
7. **Hollingbourne:** The Windmill (5 miles) — 27
8. **Egerton:** The George (3½ miles) — 30
9. **Warehorne:** The Woolpack Inn (6 miles) — 33
10. **Chartham Hatch:** The Chapter Arms (6½ or 3¾ miles) — 36
11. **Fordwich:** The Fordwich Arms (4 miles) — 39
12. **Bridge:** The White Horse Inn (3 or 6 miles) — 42

WALKS IN SURREY

13. **Tilford:** The Duke of Cambridge (7½ miles) — 45
14. **Pirbright:** The Moorhen (4 miles) — 48
15. **Ripley:** The Seven Stars (5½ miles) — 51
16. **Burrowhill:** The Four Horseshoes (3½ miles) — 54
17. **Dunsfold:** The Sun Inn (5 miles) — 57
18. **Shere:** The White Horse (7¼ miles) — 60
19. **Leatherhead:** The Running Horse (4¾ miles) — 63
20. **Walton-on-the-Hill:** The Blue Ball (5 miles) — 66
21. **Charlwood:** The Rising Sun (5¾ miles) — 69
22. **Outwood:** The Bell Inn (5¼ miles) — 72
23. **Godstone:** The Hare and Hounds (6 miles) — 75
24. **Dormansland:** The Plough Inn (4 miles) — 78

Contents

WALKS IN WEST SUSSEX

25. Bosham: The Anchor Bleu (3 miles)   81

26. Chilgrove: The White Horse Inn (7¼ miles)   84

27. Lurgashall: The Noah's Ark (4½ miles)   87

28. Duncton: The Cricketers (6¼ miles)   90

29. Amberley: The Black Horse (8 miles)   93

30. Billingshurst: The Limeburners (6¼ miles)   96

31. Partridge Green: The Partridge (6¾ miles)   99

32. Clayton: The Jack & Jill Inn (4 miles)   102

WALKS IN EAST SUSSEX

33. Fletching: The Griffin Inn (5¼ miles)   105

34. Hartfield: The Anchor Inn (7 miles)   108

35. Blackboys: The Blackboys Inn (6 miles)   111

36. East Dean: The Tiger Inn (6¾ miles)   114

37. Cowbeech: The Merrie Harriers (4½ miles)   117

38. Burwash: The Bell Inn (6½ miles)   120

39. Ewhurst Green: The White Dog Inn (4¼ miles)   123

40. Winchelsea: The Bridge Inn (5¾ miles)   126

PUBLISHER'S NOTE

We hope that you obtain considerable enjoyment from this book; great care has been taken in its preparation. However, changes of landlord and actual closures are sadly not uncommon. Likewise, although at the time of publication all routes followed public rights of way or permitted paths, diversion orders can be made and permissions withdrawn.

We cannot, of course, be held responsible for such diversion orders and any inaccuracies in the text which result from these or any other changes to the routes nor any damage which might result from walkers trespassing on private property. We are anxious though that all details covering the walks are kept up to date and would therefore welcome information from readers which would be relevant to future editions.

The simple sketch maps that accompany the walks in this book are based on notes made by the authors whilst checking out the routes on the ground. They are designed to show you how to reach the start, to point out the main features of the overall circuit and they contain a progression of numbers that relate to the paragraphs of the text.

However, for the benefit of a proper map, we do recommend that you purchase the relevant Ordnance Survey sheet covering your walk. The Ordnance Survey maps are widely available, especially through booksellers and local newsagents.

Introduction

Bodiam castle

What better way to spend a leisurely few hours than to drive into the countryside, stretch your legs and then visit a good pub for some fine food. The 40 circular walks in this book allow you to do just that. Each route, starting and finishing at a recommended pub, takes you through some of the best scenery on offer in Kent, Surrey and Sussex.

Kent, long known as the Garden of England, has wonderful walking countryside: from the coastline of white cliffs, the flat ground of north Kent and Romney Marsh, to the hills of the North Downs, Greensand Ridge and High Weald. You can stroll alongside rivers and clear streams, and through bluebell woods and colourful, blossoming fruit orchards. Kent is also rich in history and you will pass Roman villas, Norman churches, timber-framed medieval houses and Tudor and Queen Anne mansions.

Surrey, set back from the coast and once covered in near impenetrable forest, has less history of national importance than its larger neighbours. However, there is a wealth of local history contained within its small, scattered villages. In Tudor times, the king and his court ventured into the Surrey hinterland where they enjoyed hunting the deer that roamed in large quantities. In recent centuries, wealthy businessmen found that they could build large houses and estates here and commute to London.

The colourful landscape of patchwork fields separated by pretty hedgerows and small coppices makes this county a real pleasure for country walkers.

And then, there is Sussex. What a joy the county is - undulating fields, majestic woodland, soft rolling downs and jagged white chalk cliffs fronting the English Channel. Walking in Sussex is hugely popular, but many of those taking part confine themselves to the long-distance footpaths that traverse the county. A few of the walks in this book will, for a while, touch on routes such as the South Downs Way, the Sussex Border Path and the Downs Link Path but, in the main, they keep to the less well-known paths that pass through sleepy villages and pretty countryside.

Each of the 40 circular routes is between 3 and 8 miles in length. You will usually be able to park at the pub whilst doing the walk so long as you intend to call in for some refreshment. However, it is only

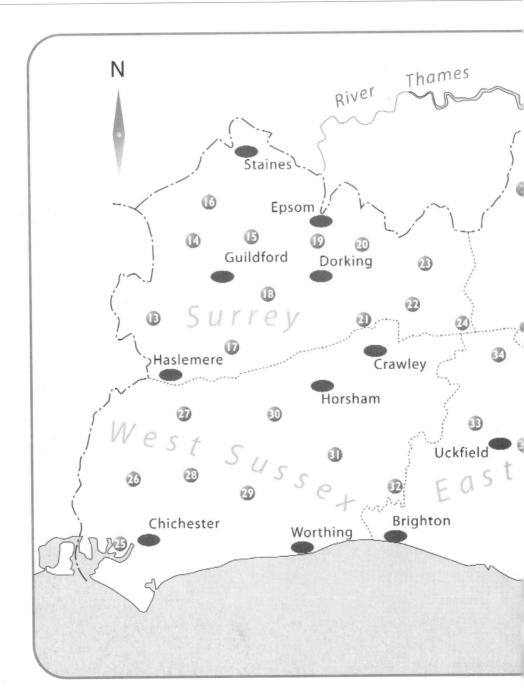

N

River Thames

Staines

16

Epsom

14   15   19   20

Guildford   Dorking   23

18

13   S u r r e y   22

17   21   24

Haslemere   Crawley   34

Horsham

27   30

W e s t   S u s s e x   33

31   Uckfield

26   28   E a s t

29   32

Chichester   Worthing   Brighton

25

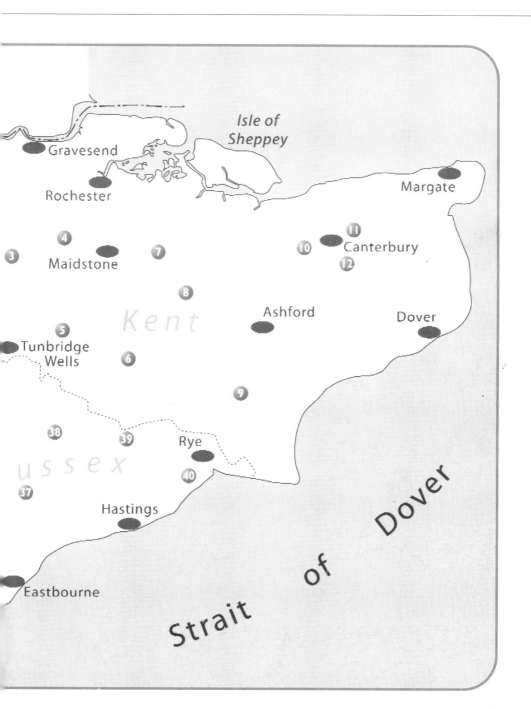

Isle of
Sheppey

Gravesend

Rochester

Margate

④

④ Maidstone

⑦

③

⑩ ⑪
Canterbury
⑫

⑧

Ashford

Dover

Kent

⑤

Tunbridge
Wells

⑥

⑨

㊳ ㊴

Rye

u s s e x

㊵

㊲

Hastings

Eastbourne

Strait of Dover

7

courteous to ask the landlord before setting out. If you prefer to use public transport some of the walks are within easy distance of a railway station. Phone National Rail Enquiries on 08457 484950 or log on to www.nationalrail.co.uk for details. All our walks are accompanied by a sketch map indicating the route to be followed. However, we strongly recommend that, for detailed information, you carry the relevant O.S. map with you. These are good value and we have given the appropriate Explorer sheet number at the start of each chapter.

To make your outing complete, a snack and a drink, together with a waterproof, packed in a rucksack will sustain you during the walk. And remember, even on the driest day there can be a muddy patch on your path. When you get to the pub it's a good idea to leave any muddy boots in the car, so don't forget to put a change of footwear in the boot before you leave home.

It just remains for us to wish you many happy hours of pleasure in following these pub walks.

Michael Easterbrook
and David Weller

On the downs above Hollingbourne

The Chafford Arms

This walk takes you through lovely undulating countryside with fine views and along a pleasant stretch on the bank of the River Medway. The river is quite narrow here as it is near to the start of its journey to the sea. The route begins at the attractive village of Fordcombe, set round a large green with its own cricket pitch. The village was largely built in 1874 by Lord Hardinge, who became Governor-General of India.

The Chafford Arms is a friendly pub in an impressive tile-hung building, with pleasant dining areas and a lovely garden. It serves a local real ale - Larkins, as well as Bass and others. There is a good range of food, including steaks and lamb chops, but the speciality is fish, bought in Hastings and including Dover sole. Lighter meals, sandwiches and ploughman's are also available.

Opening times are from 11.45 am to 3 pm and 6.30 pm to 11 pm, with food served between 12.30 pm and 2 pm and from 7.30 pm to 9.30 pm.

Telephone: 01892 740267.

Distance: *5 miles*

OS Explorer 147 Sevenoaks & Tonbridge GR 526404

A moderate walk, with some gradual slopes

Starting point: The car park of the Chafford Arms - please seek the landlord's permission to leave your car whilst walking.

How to get there: Fordcombe is 3 miles west of Tunbridge Wells and can be reached by going north from the A264 on the B2188 near Langton Green.

9

The Walk

1 Going out of the front of the pub, turn left alongside the road into the village. After 100 yards go left on a path between houses, opposite the school. Cross a stile then go diagonally left across a field to another stile near the left corner of a line of trees ahead. Turn sharp left to walk alongside a hedge on the left and with glorious views ahead. At the end of the field keep straight on over a stile, ignoring another on the left, then go diagonally right down a field to a gap between trees in the bottom right corner. Continue through this gap and along a narrow field between tall hedges to a marker post near a cottage, then left to a track. Turn right on the track to pass Palmers Farm and later reach a T-junction with a lane.

2 Turn left and continue along the lane for ½ mile then, just past a tiny church, go left on a bridleway. At the end of the churchyard, keep straight on to the left of a line of oak trees to a gate next to a metal gate. Ahead to the right you can see a plantation of the new dwarf-growing hops, with a traditional hop garden with tall poles behind. Go through the gate to walk along the right edge of a field to a metal footbridge. Don't cross it, but turn left to walk parallel with the River Medway on the near bank, going over the occasional stream by plank bridge, with several Second World War pillboxes to be seen and perhaps a kingfisher if you are

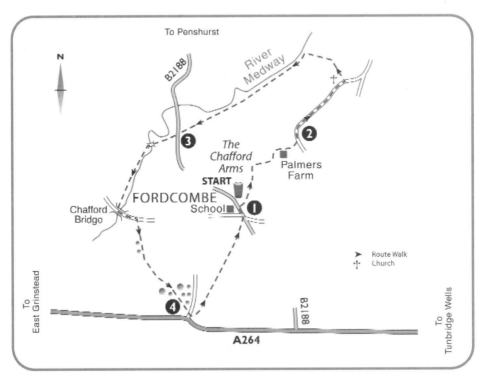

really lucky. At one point, where the river meanders to the right, keep left under power lines to rejoin it as it swings back after a few hundred yards. After crossing a footbridge with a metal handrail on its left, keep to the left edge of a field with a stream on your left and go over two stiles to a road.

3 Cross the road, with care, to a stile opposite and walk over a field to a footbridge. After crossing the river, turn left over the field to rejoin the river on its bend, then continue on the bank. Just past a sluice gate, turn left over Chafford Bridge and up a road. Ignore a drive with a footpath sign on the right and continue to another footpath sign opposite the first of some pre-fabricated bungalows on the left. Go right over the stile and along the left edge of a field, with fine views over the river valley to the right. After another stile, cross a field to the left edge of a small wood ahead, then continue with the wood and, later, a tall hedge on your right. Keep straight on through a gap in a hedge and gradually uphill to a marker post at the edge of trees, with good views to your back. Turn right into a wood and follow the path as it bends through conifers to reach a road.

4 Cross the road to a gravel drive 10 yards to the right and follow the drive as

Tranquillity along the River Medway, Fordcombe

it bends left. You are now on the Wealdway long-distance path, which takes you back to Fordcombe. After 50 yards, cross a stile on the left opposite a white-boarded house, then keep to the right edge of a succession of long fields, and finally, on a path between hedges to reach a cricket field. Go diagonally left and past the pavilion to the road and left to the pub.

Date walk completed:

....

Places of Interest

Penshurst Place & Gardens, 3 miles north of Fordcombe, is a magnificent ancestral home set amidst Tudor gardens and parkland. It has a medieval baron's hall and impressive state rooms, plus adventure playground, shop and tearoom. Telephone: 01892 870307.

Groombridge Place Gardens, 2 miles south of Fordcombe, has a series of magnificent walled gardens and a large area of ancient woodland, with adventure trails. There are also flying displays by birds of prey, a restaurant and gift shop. Telephone: 01892 863999.

Spa Valley Railway runs steam trains between Tunbridge Wells and Groombridge. Telephone: 01892 537715.

11

Eynsford

The Plough

The lovely village of Eynsford, with its old humpback bridge over the River Darent, provides a picturesque start to this walk. It also boasts an elegant church and the remains of a Norman castle. The walk reveals other aspects of the area's rich history, as it takes you past the preserved remains of a Roman villa and the Queen Anne mansion of Lullingstone Castle, with its Tudor gatehouse and tiny flint church. There are wonderful views over the scenic Darent Valley and the route also passes through Lullingstone Park, with its ancient trees and colourful downland flowers and butterflies. There is also a delightful section alongside the clear, tranquil river.

Distance: *5½ miles*

OS Explorers 162 Gravesend & Greenwich and 147 Sevenoaks & Tonbridge.
GR 541655

A moderate walk, with some gradual slopes

Starting point: The public car park in Eynsford. You can leave your car at the Plough, but please seek the landlord's permission to leave your car there whilst walking.

How to get there: From junction 3 of the M25 and M20 near Swanley, take the A20 eastwards to Farningham, then go south on the A225. The public car park is on the right in the centre of the village and just past it you turn right into Riverside to reach the Plough.

The Plough in Eynsford is in a lovely setting by the picturesque ford and bridge, where the river is popular with picnickers and paddlers in summer. There is a varied menu, including baked sea bass, lemongrass and ginger chicken with coconut rice and roasted spiced vegetables, roasted aubergine stuffed with tomato and chickpea couscous and Feta cheese. There are also steaks and lighter meals such as baguettes. The ales include Fuller's London Pride, Wadworth 6X and Boddingtons.

Opening times are 11.30 am to 11 pm Monday to Saturday, and 12 noon to 10.30 pm on Sunday, with food in the restaurant served from 12 noon to 2.30 pm and 6 pm to 9 pm on weekdays and from 12 noon to 5 pm and 6 pm to 10 pm at weekends. Bar food is available from 12 noon to 5 pm in the week, and 12 noon to 4 pm at weekends.

Telephone: 01322 862281.

The Walk

❶ From the public car park turn right and immediately right again into Riverside to go past the ford and the Plough. Keep straight on along the road where another road goes off to the right and take care along the next section as there is no footpath. Continue under a spectacular railway viaduct and past the entrance to Eagle Heights birds of prey centre. The river goes through a series of meanders on the left, often with herons fishing from the banks, and there are views to the Downs beyond.

❷ On reaching Lullingstone Roman Villa, keep straight on, but immediately past the last building on the right and before a 'Private Road' sign, go right at a signpost for the Lullingstone Park Circular Walk. Go up steps then gradually uphill through trees. Soon there are fine views back along the valley over fields on the right. Ignore a stile on the right but 100 yards after this go left through a gap in a belt of trees to a marker post, then straight on between fields. There are more views along the Darent Valley here and Lullingstone Castle is visible. Go downhill to a post with a blue ring then straight on along a track between hedges laden with blackberries and rose-hips in autumn. Continue past a golf green on the left, up a short slope into trees, then keep right where the path forks to go straight on through trees on a wide stony track. As you emerge from the trees, continue to follow the blue-ringed posts as you keep

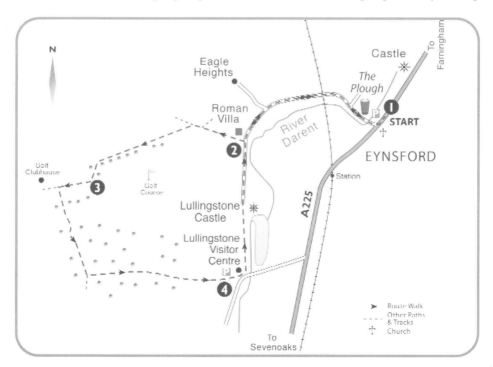

to the right-hand side of a grassy area, with oaks to your right, then on another wide track under trees. Continue on the shale track as it swings left past the huge trunk of an ancient oak tree and keep straight on at a junction of paths on the edge of a golf course. After going through more trees you emerge onto a narrow tarmac road.

❸ Turn right along the road, soon passing another ancient oak, with a hollow trunk, and near a seat for taking in the glorious view. About 200 yards before the golf clubhouse ahead to the right, go left at a tall three-armed fingerpost to cross the grass past a line of oak trees and enter a wood at a gap by a marker post. From the wood go straight across a golf fairway (with caution) to a wide grassy track, but after 40 yards go left on a narrower grassy path, which winds uphill through trees. On reaching a crossroads of paths at a fingerpost, go left on the path signposted 'Visitor Centre circular walk'. Keep to the main path, ignoring all side tracks, through woodland, along the right side of a small grassy valley, then through another wood. Later the path gets wider and goes past a wooden barrier; a few hundred yards further on, take the right fork. There are soon views ahead as the path goes down into the valley alongside a wooden post-and-rail fence to reach the Lullingstone Park Visitor Centre. This is an excellent place to obtain refreshments and get information about the wildlife of the park.

❹ Leave by the car park exit but just before the road go left through a kissing gate on the Darent Valley Path. There is now a delightful walk by the clear waters

Seen from the walk

of the river before continuing along a minor road past the impressive Tudor gatehouse of Lullingstone Castle. On reaching the Roman villa you can go straight on along the road to retrace your steps to the start.

Places of Interest

Lullingstone Roman Villa (English Heritage) has the preserved remains of several rooms of the villa, some with mosaic floors, and the bathhouse, all under cover. Telephone: 01322 863467.

Eagle Heights has many birds of prey such as eagles, hawks and owls, some used in flying displays. Telephone: 01322 866466.

Lullingstone Castle is a Tudor manor house with fine interiors and an impressive gateway. Telephone: 01322 862114.

Date walk completed:

....

14

The George and Dragon

The lovely village of Ightham, with its half-timbered houses and tile-hung cottages, provides a fine setting for the start of this walk, which takes you through some glorious countryside and past a 15th-century timbered hall house. You follow in the footsteps of ancient Britons as you walk on the heavily-wooded Oldbury Hill, an Iron Age hill-fort. There are tremendous views to the North Downs and the Greensand Ridge.

The George and Dragon is an attractive black and white timbered building, dating from the early 16th century. Inside the historic inn are fine beams and inglenook fireplaces, adding interest to the comfortable bars and restaurant, and there is also a garden. A fine selection of good food awaits you, with dishes such as organic Irish salmon with spring onion and prawn mash, plus a range of hot and cold bar snacks. Shepherd Neame ales such as Masterbrew, Spitfire and Late Red are served.

Opening times are 11 am to 11 pm on Monday to Saturday, and 12 noon to 10.30 pm on Sunday.

Telephone: 01732 882440.

Distance: 6 miles

OS Explorer 147 Sevenoaks & Tonbridge GR 594566

A moderate walk, with some gradual inclines.

Starting point: The public car park in Sevenoaks Road, Ightham.

How to get there: Ightham is on the A227, just south of the A25. Turn south by the footbridge, 1½ miles west of Borough Green, into Sevenoaks Road and the car park is on the left.

The Walk

1 Go out of the car park and turn right. (If starting from the pub, turn right from it and right again into Sevenoaks Road and past the car park.) Continue to the junction with the A25 and cross it using the footbridge on the left. Turn right and, after 50 yards, left along a lane by a white house. Where the lane bends left continue straight on.

2 Where the tarmac road ends, continue straight ahead on a bridleway to the right of a garage. The path goes up onto Oldbury Hill, ascending the ramparts of an Iron Age hill-fort - one of the largest in England. Soon orchards are visible on the right. Where the path forks at a wooden post go straight ahead (right fork). At the next path junction, by an information board, also keep straight ahead (right-hand path). At the next fork by a marker post, take the far right path ahead to go down a sunken path between tall banks with fantastic root formations. The path reaches a minor road by Styants Farmhouse.

3 Turn left along the road for 100 yards, then, just before the entrance to a camp-site, go right on a path into trees. The path skirts the camp-site then bends left uphill. At a T-junction with a bridleway go left then, just past a marker post, take the right fork. Keep straight on at a short marker post to continue on a narrower path. As you approach the A25, look for a narrow sandy cross-path before a bank ahead. Go right on this path uphill and

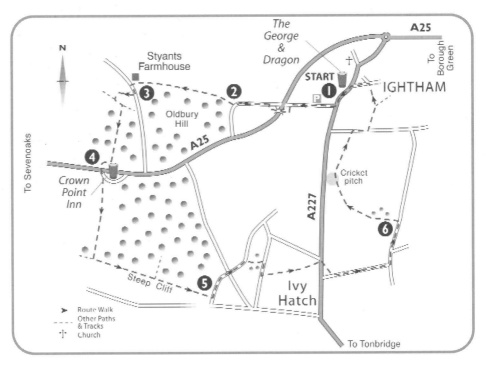

take the left fork after 50 yards to reach the A25.

4 Cross, with care, to a road opposite, leading to the Crown Point Inn. As this road bends left go straight ahead on a tarmac track to the left of a stone cottage. Continue on this track through woods until reaching a cross-track just past a wooden gate and go left. Keep on the main track but take great care here as there are sheer drops. Keep straight on where a path leaves on the left after ½ mile and continue along the top of the ridge. The path can be very muddy in places and becomes narrow between banks as it descends to a minor road.

5 Turn left along the lane to a crossroads and go straight across to another lane. Where it bends left after 200 yards go right at a fingerpost on a path to the left of a drive to reach another minor road. Turn right and go along the road for 400 yards then, at the end of a plant nursery, go left along a tarmac track. Where the tarmac ends keep straight ahead to the left of stables to reach the A227. Turn right and after 30 yards cross, with care, to a footpath sign in the hedge. Enter an orchard and go diagonally right to reach a tall hedge by a lane. Walk left alongside the hedge to a gap with a wooden barrier and turn left along the lane. At a T-junction, by a converted oast-house, turn left along another lane and keep straight on where a road goes off right.

6 Just after going under power lines go left over a stile to the left of the gate of Goddens Cottage, then left of its garage and along the left edge of the garden to continue to the left of a wood. When the wood ends, go straight on through an orchard for 50 yards to reach a concrete track and go diagonally right on it. Where it forks, keep straight on (left fork) and soon keep right of a large farmhouse, then left of a stone cottage and a ruined house. Soon, take the left fork to keep alongside trees on the left. Go through a gap in a wooden fence on the left and along the right edge of a cricket field past the pavilion; rejoin the track by going back through the fence at the far end. Continue alongside the hedge on the left, then through a gap in a windbreak, along the left edge of another orchard and down steps to a narrow road. Go right for 100 yards then left on a path at a concrete footpath sign. On reaching a T-junction with another path turn left. Go down steps to a road. Take the left fork to return to Ightham opposite the pub, then left alongside the road and right into Sevenoaks Road to the car park.

Place of Interest

Ightham Mote (National Trust), 2 miles south of Ightham, is a superb moated manor house dating from 1330 with Great Hall, Tudor chapel, garden and woodland walks. Telephone: 01732 811145.

Date walk completed:

....

West Malling

The Five-Pointed Star

This walk begins in the lovely small market town of West Malling, which has several grand houses, mainly Georgian, bordering its wide main street. It also has a Norman church with an elegant spire, medieval houses and an abbey founded in 1090. In the pleasant surrounding countryside, you will pass a stronghold tower built by the Norman bishop Gundulf, an 18th-century mansion and a fine 16th-century timbered house. The route passes through Manor Park Country Park, with its picturesque lake and fine trees and goes past fruit orchards, and oasts that were once used for drying hops.

The Five-Pointed Star is a very comfortable pub. Dating from the 14th/15th century, it has several alcoves with beams, in addition to the main bar area, while there is outdoor seating on the patio at the rear. The pub serves Greene King IPA, Ruddles County and Morland Old Speckled Hen ales. Food includes a selection of pies such as lamb, mushroom and ale and there are also mixed grills, BBQ spare ribs, chicken breast marinated in honey and mustard, and fish dishes such as rainbow trout and seafood platter. Vegetarian meals, ploughman's and jacket potatoes are also on offer.

Opening times are 10.30 am to 11 pm Monday to Friday, 9 am to 11 pm on Saturday and 12 noon to 10.30 pm on Sunday. Food is served from 10.30 am to 10 pm Monday to Friday, 9 am to 10 pm on Saturday, and from 12 noon to 10 pm on Sunday.

Telephone: 01732 842192.

Distance: *4 miles*

OS Explorer 148 Maidstone & the Medway Towns
GR 679577

An easy and mainly flat walk, apart from one short climb

Starting point: The car park of the Five-Pointed Star, but do seek the landlord's permission before leaving your car whilst you walk.

How to get there: From junction 4 of the M20, go south to the A20 then west for ½ mile to a roundabout where you go south into West Malling. The Five-Pointed Star is on the right where the street widens out. From the south, West Malling can be reached off the A228. There are both long-stay and short-stay car parks nearby.

The Walk

1 From the front of the pub, cross the main street , turn right and continue for 100 yards, then go left down Water Lane. After passing a small monastery on the left, continue for another 80 yards before turning right through a kissing gate into Manor Park Country Park. Turn right onto a gravel track which soon bends left to go alongside a lovely clear stream. The stream leads to a large lake - keep to the left of this - which has swans, coots and moorhens. Soon there is a lovely view over to the 18th-century mansion called Douce's Manor, with impressive cypress trees in its grounds. Continue on the path to the end of the lake to reach a narrow road. It is worth taking a short diversion here to view St Leonard's Tower, dating from the 11th century. Go straight across the road and past white cottages on a path leading to a road, with the tower opposite. Retrace your steps back to the narrow road. Turn left from the lake path, or right if coming back from the tower, to walk along the road or on the bank above it, to reach the car park of the country park.

2 Continue to the far end of the car park and leave it past a barrier gate. Keep to the right side of a small field to a kissing gate, then go slightly diagonally left on an obvious grassy path through parkland, with some fine trees and a view back left to West Malling church with the North Downs in the distance. As the path bends left, keep straight on, 30 yards to the right of a seat, to a kissing gate next to

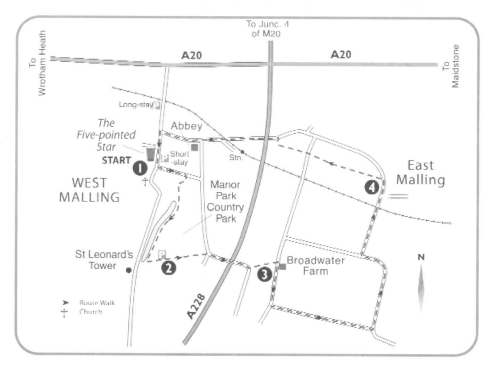

another gate. Exit to a road and go straight ahead alongside it to cross a bridge over another road. As the road bends right, go straight on through a white gate to the left of a house onto a path between apple orchards towards the white cowls atop an oast-house. Follow the path as it bends right to the right of a hedge to reach a road opposite Broadwater Farm.

3 Turn right along the narrow road then, after 400 yards take another lane on the left. This lane has tall hedges, festooned with traveller's joy (or old man's beard), and with apple and pear orchards beyond. On reaching a T-junction after ½ mile, turn left. After a few hundred yards, you pass a fine timbered house on the left. Continue on the road, past hedges with hops clambering over them, and follow it as it goes uphill and bends left. After passing houses on the right, turn right down Stickens Lane, with its blackthorn and damson hedges and banks yellow with celandines in spring. After going under a railway bridge, keep on past new houses to reach a road on a bend.

4 Turn left alongside the road and shortly past Darcy Products on the left and a half-timbered house on the right go left on a tarmac track, with a brick wall on the left. The path goes between fields, then hedges with violets on the banks in spring, to reach a road. Go straight across to a narrow path which passes more fields before reaching the end of a road, now unused. Turn right and continue for 50 yards past a metal barrier to a road. Cross with care to the footpath alongside

The Norman church at West Malling Abbey

it and turn left to follow it back into West Malling, passing the road leading to the railway station and the picturesque abbey with its water cascade. On reaching the T-junction in the centre of the town, turn left to return to the Five-Pointed Star.

Place of interest
Great Comp Garden, 4 miles west of West Malling, is a lovely 7-acre garden set around a 17th-century manor house, with many fine plants, tea room and plant sales. Telephone: 01732 886154.

Date walk completed:

....

The Bull

This walk on the High Weald goes through the heart of one of the principal fruit-growing areas of Kent, so is particularly lovely in spring when the blossom is out. Also there are tremendous views over the lower parts of the Weald. Starting in Brenchley, with its 600-year-old church and impressive half-timbered houses, the route takes you through the attractive village of Matfield. Here a delightful village green complete with duckpond and cricket pitch is bordered by picturesque cottages and an elegant 18th-century house with its own clock tower. Matfield has a total of four pubs plus an excellent tea room, and there is another pub on the route.

The Bull at Brenchley has a very comfortable interior, with secluded alcoves and log fires, and old photographs of the area add interest. There is a garden at the rear with children's play equipment and a non-smoking eating area in a conservatory. Several real ales are served, such as Greene King Abbot and IPA, Harveys, and Rebellion from the Marlow Brewery. A good selection of food is on offer, including steaks, pies and Mexican specialities such as chicken flautas. In addition, there are daily specials, mainly using fish, plus vegetarian and children's meals, and lighter snacks.

Opening times are from 11.30 am to 3 pm and 5 pm to 11 pm on Monday to Friday, 11 am to 3 pm and 6 pm to 11 pm on Saturday, and from 12 noon to 4 pm and 7 pm to 10.30 pm on Sunday. Food is served every day from 12 noon to 2.30 pm and 7 pm to 9.30 pm.

Telephone: 01892 722701.

Distance: *4 miles*

OS Explorer 136 The Weald
GR 679418

An easy, mainly flat route that can be muddy at times

Starting point: The public car park in Brenchley, adjacent to the Bull.

How to get there: Take the B2160 south from Paddock Wood or north from the A21(T) to Matfield, then at the crossroads go east for a mile to reach Brenchley. The car park is on the right, opposite the post office.

The Walk

1 Go out of the entrance to the car park and turn left along the main street. Take the right fork by the war memorial and follow it to a T-junction. Here cross 10 yards to the left, go up some steps and along the right edge of an orchard. After 200 yards, at the end of a hedge, go over a rather hidden stile on the right and continue on a path between hedges, past a fine house on the right. The path reaches a drive, where you go left past Oak Cottage to a wooden barrier fence. From here go straight on, to the left of tall alders, with orchards on both sides. Keep straight on at a marker post and at the next post keep left of a hedge, to go through a gap in a cross-hedge and along the right edge of the next orchard. Pass through another gap and go slightly diagonally left to reach a tall wire fence around a reservoir. Turn right alongside the fence to a gap in a hedge, then along the right side of an orchard with a line of trees on the right. Pass a garden on the left and go through a gap on the right, and continue in the same direction on a farm road to reach the B2160.

2 Cross, with care, and go along the drive opposite. At its end, continue to the left of a converted oast-house and on a narrower track that goes to the right of a barn, then between fields. There are wonderful views to the right over the Low Weald to the Greensand Ridge and the North Downs in the far distance. Some 10 yards before a metal gate, go diagonally right on a grassy track and past a line of tall poplars on the left to reach a cross-path. Turn left here along

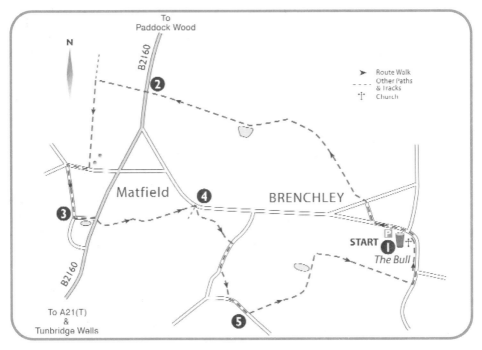

the right edge of a field, straight ahead through a gap in a hedge and to the right of scrub and between trees. At the edge of a wood, keep straight on (not left) on a narrow path through trees to reach a lane. Turn right, walk on for 200 yards. Opposite a farmhouse behind a hedge on the right, turn left down Maycotts Lane to reach Matfield village green (¼ mile).

3 Turn left onto the road before the green. On reaching the main street through the village take a path to the right of a white gate, right of Cherrytrees tea room, to go between houses then along the left edge of a field to a marker post. Continue with a hedge on the left and at the next marker post go slightly diagonally right through bushes to a stile. Continue along the left edge of an orchard but after 80 yards go left through a gap in the hedge and immediately right, to continue in the same direction with a wire fence on the right and pear orchard on the left. You soon reach a stile by a gate and then a road.

4 Turn right and after 20 yards go right down a tarmac drive. After only 5 yards, go left on a bridleway track to the left of a bungalow. This track eventually drops down to a road. Turn right, then, after 50 yards, go left at a fingerpost sign and up a bank to follow a line of telegraph poles ahead through an orchard and out onto a lane.

5 After 300 yards go left at a fingerpost along a gravel drive for Southfield Cottages to a kissing gate and on through a derelict orchard. Pass another orchard and carry straight ahead on a wider track between more orchards, towards a church in the distance. The track becomes

Matfield House and duck pond

a tarmac path and bends left past a lake. Keep straight on along a rough road and follow it as it bends right, soon with Brenchley church in view again ahead. Continue through a gate and remain on the track road, soon between farm buildings to reach a road. Go left and, 20 yards before a T-junction, take a footpath on the left to continue above the road to a churchyard. Follow the path to the right of the church to the main lychgate by cropped yews and turn left to the pub and car park.

Place of Interest

The Hop Farm Country Park, 5 miles north of Brenchley, is a family attraction with shire horses, indoor and outdoor play areas, animal farm, exhibitions and also a restaurant and gift shop. Telephone: 01622 872068.

Date walk completed:

....

23

Sissinghurst

The Bull

The historic village of Sissinghurst has several attractive buildings in typical Kentish style. This route takes you past the remains of the Tudor manor house of Sissinghurst Castle, with its world-famous gardens. The countryside through which you walk is very pleasant, with many small woods full of bluebells and wood anemones in spring. You will also see some of the fruit orchards and hop gardens which have long been a feature of this area.

Distance: 4¼ or 7 miles

OS Explorers 136 The Weald and 137 Ashford
GR 795375

An easy walk, mainly flat with some gradual slopes

Starting point: The car park of the Bull, but do seek the landlord's permission before leaving your car whilst you walk.

How to get there: From the A229, 1 mile north of Cranbrook, turn east on the A262. Sissinghurst is reached after ¾ mile, with the Bull on the left.

The Bull is in the main street in Sissinghurst and has a pleasant garden. A range of food is served, including steaks and fish dishes. There are also lighter snacks such as jacket potatoes and baguettes and children's meals. The ales include Harveys, Fuller's London Pride, Greene King IPA and Shepherd Neame Masterbrew.

Opening times are 11 am to 11 pm Monday to Saturday and 12 noon to 10.30 pm on Sunday. Food is available from 12 noon to 3 pm and 6 pm to 9 pm (12 noon to 3 pm only on Sunday).

Telephone: 01580 712821.

The Walk

1 Going out of the front of the pub, turn left along the main street and past the church. Just after a small lay-by, turn left up a tarmac drive signed with a National Trust board saying 'footpath to Sissinghurst Castle'. Where the drive ends, keep straight on along the right edge of a hop garden, over a footbridge, then go immediately right through a kissing gate into a wood. Where the track forks at a short marker post, keep straight on (right fork) and stay on the main track, muddy in places, to reach a narrow tarmac road. This is the drive to the castle and you can either turn left along it or, to avoid cars, go over a stile opposite and turn sharp left to walk alongside the road in a sheep meadow, going back to the road at the end of the field.

2 Follow the road as it bends left and, opposite the NT car park, take a path signposted to the ticket office and shop. Keep on a tarmac path between the shop and main house. Where the moat on the right ends, keep straight ahead on a grassy track along the left edge of a field. Cross a stream and keep straight on between fields to a minor road.

For the shorter walk turn left along the lane for ½ mile to a right-hand turn and rejoin the walk at Point 5 by going left on the bridleway*.

3 Turn right along the lane. After 600 yards go left where it forks. After another 300 yards turn left off the road at a stile in a gap in the hedge and go straight across the field into scrub. Go straight ahead to the right of a row of poplars and at the end of the field turn left in front of a ditch, then right over a footbridge.

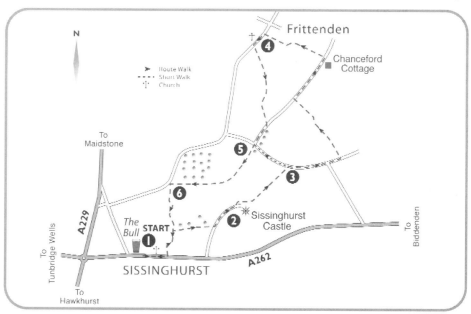

Cross the field to a stile by an oak, then across the next two fields to reach a farm track. Turn left to a minor road and turn right along it. After ½ mile, just past Chanceford Cottage, go left at a footpath sign. Go across a field to a stile next to a gate in the hedge. Continue along the right edge of two more fields to a stile among trees and into an orchard. Turn left onto a track along the left edge of the orchard and where it bends right at the end keep straight on over a stile, then go sharp right along the right edge of a field. Continue along a narrow path to a drive and turn left on the path beyond it to reach a road.

4 Turn left. Just past the Memorial Hall on the left, go left on a footpath to a stile, then across a field to a kissing gate. Continue slightly diagonally right across a large field to a gap in a hedge. Cross the plank bridge there and go straight on towards a telegraph pole. Here go diagonally right, following the line of wires to the left corner of trees. At the next pole take the path going diagonally left to reach a stile in a hedge. Continue slightly diagonally left to another stile, then maintain direction to a stile by a metal gate onto a road. Turn right along the road to reach a T-junction.

5 Go straight on here, on a tarmac drive (bridleway*) to the right of a house. Later, Sissinghurst Castle comes into view on the left. Keep straight on at cross-tracks to reach an isolated house on the right. Keep straight ahead to the left of a wood, the track becoming tarmac after passing another house.

Sissinghurst Castle

6 Just before reaching a main road, go left on a footpath past a wooden gate and along the right edge of an apple orchard. Where the grassy track and fence swing right, keep slightly left for 60 yards to a marker post at the edge of trees, then go diagonally right through an orchard on an obviously worn path between the trees. At the marker post at the far end go left, soon through trees, to the footbridge crossed on the outward journey. Keep straight on along the left edge of the hop field to the tarmac drive, then turn right when you reach the main road.

Place of Interest

Sissinghurst Castle (National Trust) is one mile east of the village and has wonderful gardens set around the lovely backdrop of the ruins of an Elizabethan mansion. Telephone: 01580 710700.

Date walk completed:

....

Hollingbourne *(Eyhorne Street)*   7 Walk

The Windmill

This walk takes you up on to the crest of the North Downs and although it is quite a steep climb you are rewarded with wonderful views over the surrounding countryside. You can also admire the colourful flowers and butterflies of the chalk downland. The villages of Hollingbourne and Eyhorne Street have several historic buildings to admire, including a 15th-century manor and an Elizabethan manor house.

The Windmill pub has a pleasant interior, with beams and a large fireplace. Parts of the building date back to the 15th century and there is a patio and large garden, with a children's play area at the rear. There is a separate restaurant and non-smoking areas. A fine menu is on offer, including dishes such as roast rack of Kentish lamb in a blackberry sauce, venison and red wine casserole, and shellfish chowder. Ales served include King & Barnes, Brakspear, Shepherd Neame Masterbrew and Flowers.

Opening hours are 11 am to 3 pm and 5 pm to 11 pm Monday to Friday; 11 am to 11 pm Saturday; and 12 noon to 10.30 pm Sunday. Food is served from 12 noon to 2.30 pm and 6 pm to 10 pm Monday to Friday; from 12 noon to 10 pm on Saturday (to 9.30 pm on Sunday).

Telephone: 01622 880280.

Distance: *5 miles*

OS Explorer 148 Maidstone & the Medway Towns
GR 833546

A challenging walk, with one steep climb

Starting point: The car park of the Windmill. Please seek the landlord's permission before leaving your car whilst you walk.

How to get there: From junction 8 of the M20 go east for ¼ mile on the A20, then north to Hollingbourne. Shortly after crossing the motorway the Windmill is reached on the right, in the part of the village known as Eyhorne Street.

The Walk

1 Going out of the front of the pub, turn right alongside the road. Where the road bends left go up the drive to Grove Mill Cottage ahead, between Cupressus hedges. Where the drive bends right, keep straight on alongside the hedge on the left and over a stile by a gate. At the end of the fence on the left, go diagonally left along the left edge of a field to another stile. Cross a footbridge, then go diagonally left across the next field and under a railway arch. Continue straight across an estate road and up a short path to a road. Turn right and soon go on a tarmac path that skirts the left edge of a recreation ground to reach a minor road near a pavilion.

2 Turn right along the road. After 600 yards, just past a lane on the right, go left at a 'Byway' sign before a house. This track goes to a T-junction with another track, the North Downs Way (NDW). Turn left onto this, with extensive views ahead and a hedge on the right laden with berries and rose-hips in autumn. Keep straight on where the track becomes a tarmac road, to reach the edge of Hollingbourne village. There is another good pub here and some fine buildings; the church is down the street to the left, which also leads back to the start should you want a shorter walk that avoids the climb to come.

3 To continue the walk, cross the road and turn right (take extreme care crossing on this short section as there is no

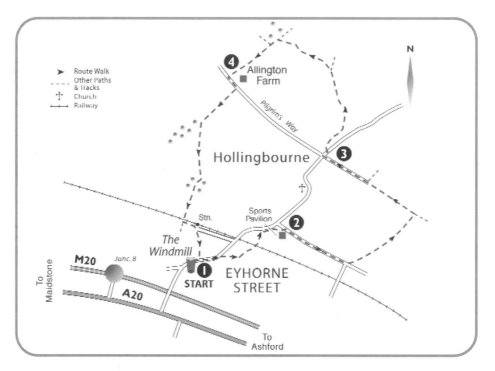

footpath). After 30 yards, go up steps on the left at a NDW sign then gradually uphill along the right edge of a field, through a kissing gate, then immediately diagonally left through a clump of bushes and up a steep slope to a marker post. Take your mind off the climb by admiring the colourful wild flowers of the chalk downland turf here - pink marjoram and centaury, mauve scabious, yellow-wort and blue harebells. At the top you are rewarded with fantastic views across to the Greensand Ridge and over the Medway Valley. Turn left at the post to go along the slope on a well-worn path which curves right after a gate. Where the path forks, keep right to go through a patch of scrub to a marker post then keep straight on to another gate, with more views of the Downs ahead. Continue between fences, with fields to the right and scrub on the left, keeping straight on at the next two gates, then through scrub and straight over a cross-track under power lines. Eventually you reach another cross-track just past a metal barrier. Turn left here by a Woodland Trust information board to go downhill on a stony track. Keep on this track for ½ mile, ignoring the NDW going off to the right, and pass a farm to emerge on a minor road.

On the North Downs Way near Hollingbourne

a grassy track between sparsely-planted oaks. The path continues across a field to a railway line. Cross, with care, then turn left immediately to a broad track. Just before a gate across the track, go right over a metal bar stile and diagonally left across a field to a gap in a hedge. Maintain direction to a stile, then follow the path to a road, where the Windmill pub is 100 yards to the right.

4 Turn left along the road. After 200 yards look for a gap in the fence on the right, marked by posts with yellow tape and rather hidden by a hedge. Cross the field, aiming for the left corner of the nearest part of the wood ahead. At the marker post there go slightly diagonally left across the field to another post at the centre of a line of trees, then continue on

Place of Interest

Leeds Castle, 1½ miles to the south of Eyhorne Street, is a lovely moated castle with superb furnishings set in a 500 acre park with gardens, aviary and a maze, plus restaurant and shops. Telephone: 01622 765400.

Date walk completed:

....

29

Egerton

The George

Perched on the Greensand Ridge that crosses the centre of Kent, Egerton is a pleasant village with a fine 14th-century church, built of ragstone and with a magnificent tower that can be seen for miles around. It makes a particularly attractive sight in spring, when the blossom of the fruit trees in the surrounding orchards is at its best. The walk goes through several of these orchards and has lovely views over the pleasant countryside of the Kentish Weald, scenery that featured in *The Darling Buds of May* and subsequent books of H. E. Bates, who lived in this area.

The George pub, a fine white weatherboarded building in the centre of the village, dates from the 16th century and has beams and real fires. It serves a good selection of ales including Greene King Abbot, Ruddles, Shepherd Neame Masterbrew and Fuller's London Pride. A wide range of food includes steaks, mixed grill, lasagne, Sunday roasts and a children's menu and there is a separate restaurant and a garden.

Opening times are 12 noon to 11 pm Monday to Saturday and 12 noon to 10.30 pm on Sunday. Food is served from 12 noon to 2 pm and 7 pm to 9.30 pm except for Sunday and Monday evenings.

Telephone: 01233 756304.

Distance: *3¼ miles*

OS Explorer 137 Ashford
GR 907473

An easy walk with some gradual slopes

Starting point: The public car park at the village hall in Egerton.

How to get there: From the A20 between Lenham and Charing turn south to Charing Heath, then continue south to Egerton. The George is on the left. Turn left after the pub and immediately right to reach the village hall car park.

The Walk

1 Take in the magnificent view from the village hall car park, then walk to the George and continue up the main street towards the church. Go left into the churchyard and follow a path around the church and down into a dip where there is a wooden gate with a Greensand Way arrow. You will be following this long-distance path for the first part of the walk. Continue ahead through an apple orchard, going slightly diagonally right. In spring the trees are covered with pink and white blossom, creating a lovely view back to the church. After 200 yards the path curves right then left and later goes to the right of a copse of trees and along the left edge of an orchard to a metal gate. Go through a narrow belt of trees

then ignore a stile in front but go straight ahead on a wide path between tall poplars on the right and a hedge on the left. After a stile by a metal gate continue past cottages to a minor road.

2 Go straight across the road to a stile, with fine views ahead over the Weald. Cross the field by going slightly diagonally right to a stile in a dip in the far right corner then down steps, through trees, and straight across a field to another stile. Continue for 20 yards along the right edge of another field then turn right over a stile and go diagonally left across a narrow field to a post at the far right corner. The path goes into hazel coppice and crosses a stream by a plank bridge, then through trees and over another stream to a stile. Continue right

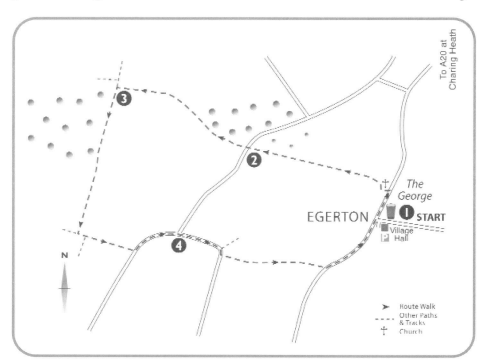

31

Far reaching views over the Weald

for 30 yards to a further stile, then along the left edge of a field to a stile in the far left corner.

3 Leave the Greensand Way here by turning left on a track that goes through the edge of a wood and later between hedges, with fields beyond. Where the hedge on the right ends by a metal gate, cross a stile and go straight ahead along the left edge of a field. At the end of the field go left through a gateway, ignore a stile on the right, and go slightly diagonally left across a large field, aiming for a house with conservatory in the distance. Cross a stile by a gate, then turn left onto a minor road past Star & Garter Cottage and continue uphill.

4 Take a narrow lane on the right just

before a stone cottage and look back for a great view. Pass the half-timbered Bedewell on the left then, as the lane bends right, ignore the first footpath sign on the bend but take the footpath at a second sign, a few yards on. The path goes through two sets of double gates by stables and alongside a hedge on the left side of a field to a stile. Continue along the left edge of the next field to another stile by a gate, then keep to the right edge of the next field to a metal gate in the far right corner. Continue on a track past barns to reach a road then go left on its verge to return to the pub and car park.

Date walk completed:

....

Place of Interest
Leeds Castle, 7 miles to the west of Egerton, is a lovely moated castle with superb furnishings. It is set in a 500-acre park and has gardens, aviary and a maze, plus restaurant and shops. Telephone: 01622 765400.

The Woolpack Inn

This circuit takes you through the unique, atmospheric scenery of Romney Marsh. As you walk beside the tranquil Royal Military Canal, built between 1804 and 1809 to guard against possible invasion by Napoleon, you may see a variety of wildlife, including the now endangered water-vole.

Distance: *6 miles*

OS Explorer 125 Romney Marsh
GR 989326

A largely moderate, flat walk with a gradual climb; the woods can be muddy

Starting point: The car park at the Woolpack Inn. Please obtain permission from the landlord to leave your car there whilst on the walk.

How to get there: From the A2070 south of Ashford turn off to Hamstreet, then turn right onto the B2067 and 1 mile to the west turn left to Warehorne.

You pass ancient churches and enjoy magnificent views over the marshes to the coast.

The Woolpack dates back to the 16th century and reflects this long history by having a smugglers' tunnel, which led to the church. A fine selection of food is served, including dishes such as Kentish shoulder of lamb topped with garlic breadcrumbs and bacon lardons with red wine gravy, steaks and lighter meals and snacks. Several real ales are available, including Goachers, Adnams and Timothy Taylor.

Opening times are 11.30 am to 3 pm and 6 pm to 11 pm Monday to Saturday and 12 noon to 3.30 pm and 7 pm to 10.30 pm on Sunday. Food is served from 12 noon to 2.30 pm and 6.30 pm to 9.30 pm Monday to Saturday and 12 noon to 3 pm and 7 pm to 9 pm on Sunday.

Telephone: 01233 733888.

The Walk

1 Going out of the pub turn left down the road past the church and follow it until you reach the Royal Military Canal. There are good views along the canal from the bridge here and, as you go left along the near bank, there are also fine views back to Warehorne.

2 When you reach a busy, fast road cross with care and continue on the opposite bank of the canal. You soon cross another road, then there is a further stretch of 1½ miles alongside the canal, with views over the surrounding flat land of Romney Marsh. Notice how at intervals there are bends in the canal - these were constructed so that guns could fire along sections of the waterway in the

event of a French invasion. This is a good area for spotting wildlife, with yellow water-lilies and other flowers in and alongside the canal, as well as the burrows of water-voles. While walking here on a sunny winter's day, as well as swans and a heron I saw the blue flash of a kingfisher and two pure-white little egrets fishing. The lovely church at Ruckinge, dating back to Norman or possibly Saxon times eventually comes into view. When you get level with it, turn left along a narrow road over a concrete bridge and into the village.

3 Turn right at the T-junction, past the Blue Anchor pub, and after 200 yards turn left up a road to Turves Farm. Keep on this drive as it curves to the right of the farmhouse and look back for a

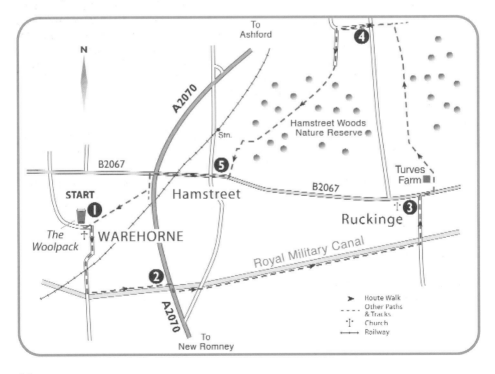

wonderful view over Romney Marsh to the sea. Where the drive ends, go through a metal gate and diagonally left up a field to a stile by a gate in the far left corner, with more views back to Dungeness and along the old coastline to the right. Continue along the left edge of a field and through another gate, then ahead on a wide grassy track along the edge of a wood. Where the wood ends, keep straight on along a sunken grassy track and over two stiles next to gates (ignore stiles on the left). On reaching a cross-track, turn left to soon reach a road.

4 Go straight across and along Poundhurst Road until it bends right, where you go left along Gill Lane. You are now on the Greensand Way long-distance path and will be following it for the next part of the walk. Keep straight on past a white farmhouse and a lovely oast-house until you reach an information board for Hamstreet Woods National Nature Reserve. Take the extreme right track of three and at the next gate, and information board, keep to the right fork. You are unlikely to see the rare moths for which the reserve is famous but you may spot speckled wood, brimstone and white admiral butterflies, or be lucky enough to hear nightingales singing between April and June. Keep to the main track and take the left fork at the next Greensand Way marker post and later a right fork, keeping straight over any cross-tracks. After ¾ mile of woodland walking you reach a T-junction, with a stony cross-track at the edge of the wood. Go left on this track to reach a large information board, then

right for a few yards over a stream to the end of a road by houses. Turn left down the road and on reaching a T-junction turn right.

5 You soon reach a crossroads by the Duke's Head pub in the centre of Hamstreet. Go straight across and past a Wealden hall-house and some attractive cottages. Where the footpath ends, take extreme care as you walk along the road under a railway arch and along the next section with no footway. Twenty yards past an overhead road crossing go left at a stile by a Saxon Shore Way sign, up steps and along a path between trees and a wire fence. After 200 yards turn right over a stile (towards a church in the distance) keeping to the right edge of the first field to another stile then slightly diagonally left across the next one. Continue along the left edge of two more fields to a footbridge, then the right edge of fields to reach a tarmac road by houses. Keep ahead to a minor road opposite Warehorne church, with the Woolpack Inn to the right.

Place of Interest

The South of England Rare Breeds Centre is 3 miles west of Warehorne and has friendly farm animals, a large playground, toddlers' paddling pool, woodland walks and restaurant. Telephone: 01233 861493.

Date walk completed:

....

Chartham Hatch

The Chapter Arms

This walk could be done in one long stretch or as two loops on separate occasions. The first loop takes you to the lovely village of Chartham, with its ancient church and picturesque green surrounded by fine houses. There is also a short but scenic section alongside the River Great Stour. The second loop goes through woodland and past Bigbury Hill, an Iron Age hill-fort reputed to be the site of a battle between ancient Britons and Caesar's invading Roman army. Both loops pass through orchards old and new.

The **Chapter Arms** has been an inn for over 100 years, having formerly been a farm belonging to the Deans (or Chapter) of Canterbury Cathedral, hence its unusual name. The inn has a spacious, comfortable interior and a large, pleasant garden. The extensive menu includes such treats as honey roast lamb in a port and rosemary gravy. There are also lighter meals and baguettes. Shepherd Neame Masterbrew and Late Red and Harveys ales are served, plus lagers and ciders.

Opening times are from 12 noon to 3 pm and 6.30 pm to 11 pm, with food served from 12 noon to 2 pm and 7 pm to 9 pm.

Telephone: 01227 738340.

Distance: *6½ or 3¼ miles*

OS Explorers 150 Canterbury & the Isle of Thanet and 149 Sittingbourne & Faversham
GR 103565

A moderate walk with some climbs

Starting point: The car park of the Chapter Arms; please seek the landlord's permission before leaving your car whilst you walk.

How to get there: From the A28, 2 miles west of Canterbury turn north on Howfield Lane to Chartham Hatch and take the first minor road on the left (New Town Street). The pub is a few hundred yards on the right.

The Walk

1 From the front of the pub turn right along the lane. At the bottom of the hill turn left at a stile by a footpath sign and along a track between apple and plum orchards. Go through a gap in a hedge then take the right fork where the path divides. Go diagonally right across a field to a stile, up a bank to another, then diagonally left across the next field. On reaching a minor road turn left and walk to the main road.

2 Cross the busy road with great care and continue ahead into Chartham. Turn right in front of the church, built in 1294 of bonded flint, to the village green. On reaching the bridge over the Great Stour, turn right into Riverside to walk alongside the river. Cross the railway line with care. The 14th-century Deanery is across fields to your left.

3 On reaching the A28 again, cross with care and turn right for 100 yards, then go left at a stile to cross a long field, aiming for a telephone mast ahead. At the top of the field turn right to a road and left onto it to cross another railway line then, 15 yards further on, go over a stile on the left into Grandma's Orchard. Keep to the right side of the orchard to walk parallel to the road. Continue through the right edge of the orchard and where a second fence starts on the right go to the right of it to get back to the road and turn left onto it.

4 After ¼ mile turn left along a drive

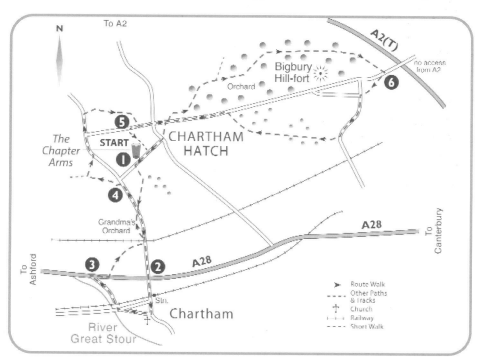

between a white house and a converted oast-house, then on a gravel track behind the oast-house. Just past a greenhouse and pond go left by a metal gate, then immediately right behind a garage and along a track with orchards on the left. At a T-junction with a concrete track turn right on the track to reach a road. Turn left along it and, where it forks, keep straight on along Primrose Hill. Just past a house on the left with a tall TV mast turn right on a track just before a wooden garage. At a marker post 15 yards further on keep straight on and follow the track for ¼ mile to reach a minor road. *For the shorter walk, turn right for 100 yards then left at a stile by a white gate and along the right edge of a plum orchard to reach the pub.*

5 To continue the longer walk, turn left along the road and at a crossroads go straight across into Bigbury Road. After 200 yards, go left at a North Downs Way (NDW) sign, going between bungalows, then right into a recreation ground and along its right edge to enter a wood. Keep straight on along the main track, following the NDW markers. After you have gone along the left edge of No Man's Orchard, go diagonally left on a cross-track at a marker post onto a sandy path. Keep to the main path on the right where it forks, then left at the next fork (still NDW). Close by is Bigbury Camp. You eventually leave the wood and reach a minor road.

6 Go straight across the road and up steps to a stile, then along the right edge of an orchard to another road. Turn left

Chartham church

and after 10 yards take the left fork. Where this road bends sharp left, go straight on at a signpost on a path between fences. Keep on this path, ignoring a stile on the left until you pass the large ornamental pond at Little Howfield Farm and go up a dirt road to a minor road. Turn left to return to Chartham Hatch. At the footpath sign opposite the recreation ground go left on a path between gardens to a road. Cross to the path and turn left for 80 yards then take the right fork to shortly reach the Chapter Arms.

Place of Interest

There are numerous attractions in Canterbury, 3 miles to the east, including **Canterbury Roman Museum** telephone 01227 785575.

Date walk completed:

....

The Fordwich Arms

The pretty village of Fordwich was once an important port on the River Great Stour, and the place where Caen stone for the building of Canterbury Cathedral was unloaded. You can still see England's smallest town hall here, a lovely timbered building with red bricks in a herring-bone pattern, and there are many attractive houses and cottages, plus a delightful church. The walk takes you through woods that are alive with birdsong and full of bluebells and other wild flowers in spring. A fine view along the river valley can be seen.

Distance: 4 miles

OS Explorer 150 Canterbury & the Isle of Thanet
GR 181598

An easy, mainly flat walk with a few gradual climbs; can be muddy in places

Starting point: The car park of the Fordwich Arms; please obtain the landlord's permission to leave your car whilst you walk.

How to get there: Fordwich is 2 miles north-east of Canterbury. Turn south from the A28 at Sturry and Fordwich is reached after ¼ mile.

The Fordwich Arms is in a fine position next to the old town hall and alongside the river. It offers meals such as cider braised beef, lamb with tomato, red wine and rosemary, rich venison pudding and rabbit in ale. Bar snacks and meals are available in comfortable and friendly surroundings. A range of real ales is served, including Wadworth 6X, Flowers Original, Whitbreads and Boddingtons.

Opening times are 11 am to 11 pm Monday to Saturday and 12 noon to 3 pm and 7 pm to 10.30 pm on Sunday.

Telephone: 01227 710444.

The Walk

❶ From the pub and town hall go straight ahead for 50 yards between a tall brick wall on the right and white cottages, then turn left down the very narrow School Lane. The first part of the walk follows the long-distance Stour Valley Walk. The lane soon becomes a path between gardens, leading to a stile, after which you cross a small field to another. Continue along the left edge of a succession of fields in which various trees are being grown as a crop, some with lovely colours in autumn. On the left is a ditch, with reedbeds and lakes beyond. Enter a wood at a stile and keep straight ahead on the main path through it, with fine displays of bluebells and other flowers in spring. Keep straight on at a

cross-track and past the massive trunk of an ancient sweet chestnut, the tree species which makes up most of the wood. After ¾ mile of woodland walking, where the path forks, go straight ahead up a bank at a marker post to a stile out of the wood. Keep to the left edge of a field, with fine views along the Stour Valley, its lakes glinting blue on a sunny day. At the end of the field is a track leading to the Flemish-style Higham Farm.

❷ Turn right onto the track to reach a minor road and cross it to a stile, then walk ahead on a wide track and into a wood. Just after the track bends left past log piles, take the right fork to go down a slope, with a tall wire fence on the right surrounding a pheasant-breeding compound. Go straight on at a cross-

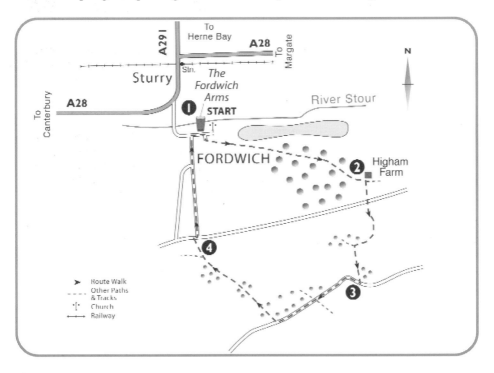

track and over two streams to a stile to the right of a wide metal gate. Turn sharp right to walk alongside the stream to another stile to the left of a gate. Go sharp left after this along the left edge of a field, later with a wood on the left where oak, beech and birch provide leaf colour in autumn, to reach a minor road.

❸ Turn right along the lane, first between hedges, then with a wood on the right. There follows a ¾ mile stretch along this quiet road, with woodland flowers and birdlife to admire. Continue past footpaths leaving on both sides until, just before a metal fence on the right, where the wood opens out, you will see a marker post set back in the woodland. Go right here through a section of woodland, then diagonally left across an open area to a disused tarmac road. Turn right onto the road, which soon becomes a dirt track, and where it bends left, keep straight on at a marker post. The path goes through a sweet chestnut wood to a plank bridge then across a field, just to the right of telegraph poles, to enter another wood. Keep on the main track through chestnut coppice, later under telegraph wires, with a field behind bushes on the right. Keep straight on where a track goes off left just before a wooden stable and continue past a metal gate to reach a minor road.

❹ Cross to a narrow lane slightly to the right and follow it between fields, then between high banks topped with fine trees, to reach Fordwich. Continue

The church at Fordwich

straight ahead down the main street to where it bends left, where you turn right to return to the Fordwich Arms.

Place of Interest
Three miles north of Fordwich, off the A291, is Wildwood, where wildlife such as otters, badgers, wolves and beavers can be seen. It also has an adventure playground. Telephone: 01227 712111.

Date walk completed:

....

The White Horse Inn

This walk starts in Bridge, a village with three pubs, a restaurant and a bakery. It takes you through the lovely Elham Valley, where the Nailbourne, a beautifully clear chalk stream, flows through rolling downland. Stately mansions are surrounded by attractive parkland with fine trees, and there are some ancient churches. For those interested in railway history, there are glimpses of the railway which ran along the valley but closed in 1947. There is also a section through woodland and along quiet lanes, both full of wild flowers in spring.

The White Horse Inn is an attractive 500-year-old building standing in the High Street. It has a very comfortable interior, with spacious bars, a large inglenook fireplace and a pleasant restaurant area. A large garden is at the rear. Four real ales are always available, such as Shepherd Neame Masterbrew, Adnams, Abbots and Black Sheep from the Masham brewery, while several wines are available by the glass. A fine selection of food is served in the restaurant and in the bars. Examples include local sea bream braised in a red wine jus with potatoes, shallots and salsify, pan-fried duck breast on honey roast parsnips and chicory; and roasted loin of venison with celeriac puree and port gravy. Lighter meals and baguettes are also available.

Distance: 3 or 6 miles

OS Explorers 150 Canterbury & the Isle of Thanet and 138 Dover, Folkestone & Hythe
GR 183543

The shorter walk is easy apart from one gradual climb; the longer route involves a longer, steeper climb

Starting point: The car park of the White Horse, but please seek the landlord's permission before leaving your car whilst you walk.

How to get there: Bridge is just off the A2, 3 miles south-east of Canterbury. Going south from the A2 into the village, the White Horse is on the left.

Opening times are 11 am to 3 pm and 6 pm to 11 pm Monday to Saturday; 12 noon to 3 pm and 6 pm to 10.30 pm on Sunday. Food served from 12 noon to 2.30 pm and 6.30 pm to 9.30 pm.

Telephone: 01227 830249.

The Walk

1 Going out of the pub, turn left up the main street. Just past the church turn right into Bourne Park Road. After 100 yards, go over a stile on the left and take the right-hand of two footpaths. You are on the Elham Valley Way, a long-distance footpath along the valley, and will be following it for the first part of the walk. The path gradually veers away from the lane to a tall marker post at the left edge of a small wood that juts out into the field. Keep straight on alongside the wood to a stile into another small wood. Go left through the trees to rejoin the lane and turn left, soon with views of Bourne Park, a superb Queen Anne mansion built in 1702. About 100 yards past its entrance gate go right over a stile and diagonally left, to the left of a lake, and maintain direction, aiming for a church in the distance. Cross a stile in a fence then footbridges over two lovely clear streams. After the second, turn sharp left to a stile at the left edge of the churchyard wall, go through the churchyard to the lychgate and out onto a lane.

2 *For the shorter walk, turn right along the lane to go over the disused Elham Valley Railway. The lane bends right, then left, and after a further 250 yards, go right at a footpath sign to rejoin the longer walk at Point 4.* To continue the longer walk turn left onto the lane and continue for 20 yards then take the right fork into Bishopsbourne, whose Mermaid Inn is renowned for its real ales. Continue to where the road bends left and go

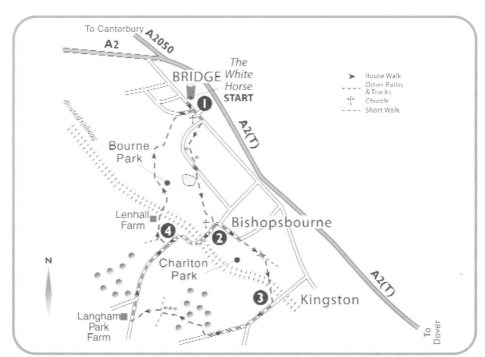

straight ahead on a tarmac track to the left of a brick cottage. The track takes you through some lovely parkland with soon some fine views of the white Tudor mansion of Charlton Park. Where the drive to the house bends right, keep straight on through a metal gate, signed 'Bridleway to Kingston'. After a few hundred yards, cross a small brick bridge over a stream and go through another gate. Leave the Elham Valley Way here by going right for 50 yards to the end of a fence on the left, then diagonally left across a large field. You reach an embankment, ascended by steps, of a disused railway which has become an unofficial linear nature reserve. Go straight across and down steps, then diagonally left across a field and between gardens to reach a road opposite White Locks farmhouse.

❸ Turn right to go uphill, with fine views over the valley as you get higher. Keep right where the road forks, then after ¼ mile a wood comes down to the road on the right. At the top of a rise turn right into the wood at a bridleway sign. Go straight over a cross-track a few yards in to keep on a wide track. The path is not waymarked through the wood, so keep left where the track forks to keep to the left edge of the wood under conifers. It then bends right, with conifers on the left. After 100 yards take the right fork, which soon goes downhill, across a cross-track, and into a narrow belt of dense conifers. Emerge from these to continue with a field to the left and trees to the right. Where these trees end, go right for 30 yards then left on an earth track between fields to a lane. Turn right past

Langham Park farmhouse and a bank of exposed chalk with caves on the right. Keep straight on where another lane joins from the left and continue for ¾ mile. Just past two large houses on the left go left at a footpath sign.

❹ Keep alongside trees around a garden to a short marker post, then left for 30 yards. Where the hedge bends away left go diagonally right (not straight on) across a large field, aiming for the cowls of an oast-house. At a T-junction of farm roads ahead turn right across a bridge and follow the stony track as it bends left. Keep on past a white cottage, a hop garden and a stone house. Another 150 yards on go left at a stile by a footpath sign and slightly diagonally right across a field to a gate at the far right corner. Keep to the right edge of the next field alongside a stream. The impressive house on the far bank is Bridge Place, the surviving part of a 17th-century mansion. Just before a pond, cross footbridges over two streams on the right and cross a small field to a lane. Go right along it to reach the main street in Bridge, with the White Horse Inn to the left.

Place of Interest

Higham Park, just south of Bridge, is a beautiful mansion, with lovely Italianate gardens and a tea lawn. Telephone: 01227 830830.

Date walk completed:

....

The Duke of Cambridge

This exhilarating walk is eminently suitable at any time of year. The circuit starts alongside the manicured landscape of Tilford golf course before turning by peaceful Stockbridge Pond and heading out into the wilder reaches of Hankley Common. Keeping mainly to low ground, the way skirts both Yagden and Kettlebury Hills as it heads for Rushmoor and then on to Frensham Little Pond, where it follows the water's edge for a while. The way then continues on a wide sandy track through oak woodland before it eventually meets up again with Stockbridge Pond.

The Duke of Cambridge is a comfortable freehouse which draws its customers from far and wide, attracted no doubt by the good food. The lunchtime and evening menus offer great choices that range from appetisers such as warm garlic ciabatta bread through to main courses in the evening that include pot roasted lamb rump on parsley mashed potatoes with caramelized shallots. A good selection of sandwiches and jacket potatoes is also available.

Opening times are from 11 am to 11 pm each day (12 noon to 10.30 pm Sundays) with food being served between 12 noon and 2.30 pm and 6.30 pm until 9.30 pm.

Telephone: 01252 792236.

Distance: *7½ miles*

OS Explorer 145 Guildford and Farnham GR 876425

An easy walk on fairly level ground

Starting point: The pub car park. Please obtain permission to leave your car. Alternative Parking: Stockbridge Pond car park, ¼ mile north of the pub (GR 875430).

How to get there: From the A3 at Milford go through Elstead and follow signs to Tilford. Go left at Tilford and the Duke of Cambridge will be found after ½ mile.

The Walk

1 From the Duke of Cambridge, walk along a small lane beside the pub to reach a golf club. Turn left through a car park and keep ahead on a bridleway that runs alongside the first tee and fairway. Soon you reach Stockbridge Pond, where you should continue leftwards around the water's edge to meet a T-junction with a wide track.

2 Turn right to soon meet a vehicle barrier. Pass by the barrier and in 80 yards, at a junction of tracks, bear left on the main track to reach an open sandy area after 80 yards. Here, at a fork, go right on a rising track between stands of pine and soon keep left at another fork. This sandy path now offers fine views over the heath. At a large junction of tracks keep ahead and soon, as you meet more tracks, again keep ahead now with power cables in front of you. This wide track skirts Yagden Hill and remains parallel to the line of cables to your left.

3 With the power cables crossing an area of open marshy grassland to your left you should keep ahead and after 100 yards, at a fork, bear left on a slowly rising bridleway that now passes under the cables. On a downward slope bear right at a fork and pass under the cables. Soon the track is joined by another and our route continues ahead to meet a small tarmac road.

4 Ahead through the trees you will spot a building used by the army, who train

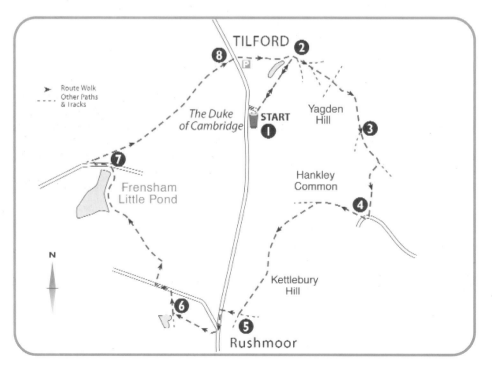

over this open area. Our way is rightwards here until we take a bridleway sign (numbered 101). The bridleway goes up an incline between banks and soon passes old concrete fortifications. Before long we see the golf course ahead of us and just before we meet it you should bear off to the left. Maintain direction now until after going over the crest of Kettlebury Hill you bear rightwards at a fork. Go over a crossing track and press on ahead as our route is joined by another track.

5 At a large junction of tracks by an MoD sign turn right down a small gully, where you soon meet a road. Turn left along the road and immediately after crossing Sandy Lane, turn right onto an enclosed footpath. At the end of gardens bear right on a public footpath alongside a fence. Lovely open views to The Devil's Jumps on your right will be seen from here. Keep to this path until it ends at a T-junction with a bridleway with a heathland pool ahead of you.

6 Turn right along the bridleway to meet a road. Go left along the road and then turn right onto a bridleway alongside the gate to a house named Firwood. The track follows the edge of the garden and brings you to a small driveway. Turn left here and, ignoring a path to your right and a fork to your left, keep ahead beside a field. The path becomes enclosed here and our route is along it. Later ignore a path on your left and keep ahead until you meet the waters of Frensham Little Pond. Press on around the bank of the

pond and cross a small planked bridge to soon meet a road.

7 Turn left along the road and when you meet low metal railings on your left turn right on a path that brings you to public conveniences. Go right here on the larger track that is closest to the toilets. This lovely track offers you easy walking as it leads you through pretty oak woodland. Remain on this track until you finally reach a road.

8 Cross the road and pass Stockbridge Pond car park. If you parked here, this marks the end your walk, but to return to the pub continue along the wide track until the pond is met. Here turn right along the bridleway and retrace your steps to the Duke of Cambridge and the end of this great walk.

Place of Interest
The Rural Life Centre is ½ mile west of Tilford in Reeds Road, and claims to be the biggest countryside collection in the south of England. This private collection covers 10 acres and displays farming implements and village life through the ages. It is open from April to September, 11 am to 6 pm, on Wednesdays and Sundays. Telephone: 01252 792300.

Date walk completed:

....

The Moorhen

What a joy the village of Pirbright is - a superb green, a pretty duck pond, many old houses, two good pubs and, tucked away down a small lane, the granite obelisk marking the last resting place of the much travelled journalist, Henry Morton Stanley. This easy to follow and level circuit contains many wide tracks that make it ideal for family groups of all ages and abilities. Passing through lovely woodland containing pine, birch and chestnut the route reaches Stamford Common. As the circuit makes its way back towards Pirbright it continues through more magnificent woodland and along a quiet lane before soon reaching the village green and the end of the walk.

The **Moorhen** was once known as the White Hart, renamed after a recent facelift. All tastes are catered for with vegetarians having a good choice and children their own menu. The draught beers include Bass, London Pride and Tetley's Cream Flow. During the summer the large and well kept garden makes a very pleasant place to sit.

Opening times are from 12 noon until 11 pm each day (Sunday 10.30 pm). Food is served between 12 noon and 10 pm (Sunday 9.30 pm) with a dining area large enough to alleviate the need to book.

Telephone: 01483 799715.

Distance: *4 miles*

OS Explorer 145 Guildford and Farnham GR 946559

An easy walk on level ground

Starting point: The Moorhen car park. Please obtain permission to leave your car. Alternatively, park in lay-bys around the village green.

How to get there: Pirbright is 5 miles south-west of Woking and sits on the A324.

The Walk

1 With the pub at your back, cross the A324 and continue ahead passing a timber-framed house named Hatchers. At a small road junction go left along the road, where you soon glimpse Stanley's obelisk over the wall of St Peter's graveyard. After passing the church and rounding a bend go left over a stile by a field gate. Go ahead now along the left-hand side of two fields and continue along a short enclosed path that ends at Mill Lane.

2 Turn right along this quiet rural lane until a junction of lanes is met. Go left here on a potholed track and ignore a footpath later on your right. Soon after this pretty track dips between banks our route goes leftwards at a fork. When the track suddenly ends, press on ahead on a narrower path through trees. After crossing a small planked bridge over a stream, exit the woodland and go ahead through a small meadow. Soon re-enter more woodland and cross a second stream; by maintaining direction ahead the route meets a T-junction.

3 Turn right here along the bridleway and continue until it ends at a T-junction soon after passing a couple of isolated houses. Turn right along the wide track that now borders the army training grounds. By a military gateway, turn right and after 20 yards go left on a pretty path between birch, chestnut and oak trees. Maintain direction ahead and soon re-join the wide track, which leads us

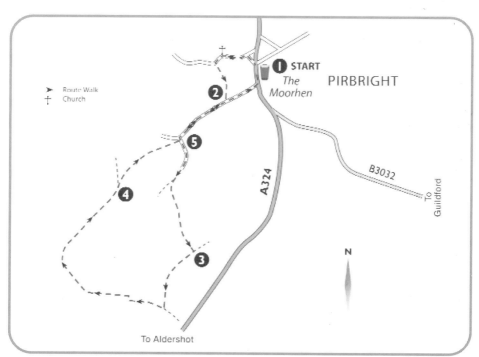

Some of the peaceful woodland near Pirbright

rightwards. Remain on this lovely track that edges this seemingly unspoilt heath to your left.

❹ When the track divides by another military gate keep to the right fork on a downhill slope through woodland. After 200 yards pass by a gate and keep ahead as we meet another track. Soon, at a junction of paths, bear left onto a broad farm track that follows a line of power cables. As the track widens we pass half a dozen houses and soon find ourselves back at Mill Lane.

❺ The route now takes us to the far end of the lane, where it meets the A324. Cross the main road and turn left along the pavement where we pass a row of Victorian houses and soon meet up with the Moorhen, and the end of a very fine walk.

Place of Interest

Guildford Castle in Castle Street, Guildford, is Surrey's only royal castle. Built during the 12th century on an older Norman motte and bailey, it became the centre of the county's administration and justice. Guildford Borough Council bought the ruins in 1885 and since then has laid out pretty gardens in the grounds. The castle is not open to the public, but the grounds are open daily from 7.30 am until dusk. Telephone: 01483 444718.

Date walk completed:

....

The Seven Stars

This lovely walk starts by following the towpath of the River Wey Navigation. In the past, barges transported coal upstream from London through twelve locks to outlying Surrey villages, while wood, farm produce and flour milled at riverside mills made the return journey. Nowadays, the craft in their retirement are crewed by pleasure seekers who enjoy the solace these quiet waters offer.

The Seven Stars has a garden for summer use and open fires during winter and provides good home cooked food. Sandwiches through to a more substantial wild sea trout dish are offered. Beers include London Pride, Abbot Ale and Old Speckled Hen plus a changing guest beer.

Distance: *5½ miles*

OS Explorer 145 Guildford and Farnham
GR: 039569

An easy walk on level ground

Starting point: The Seven Stars car park. Please obtain permission to leave your car. Alternatively, use the small free car park 200 yards from the pub (GR 039573).

How to get there: Take the B367 from the centre of Ripley and the pub will be met after ½ mile.

Opening times are from 12 noon to 3.30 pm and 6 pm to 11 pm (10.30 pm on Sundays). Cooked food is served from 12 noon to 2 pm and 6 pm to 9 pm. Booking on summer weekends is essential.

Telephone: 01483 225128.

The Walk

1 With the pub behind you, turn left and at the end of a tall yew hedge continue on a path that runs parallel to the road. Pass alongside a small wooded car park (the alternative parking) and soon cross a road bridge. Within yards, when opposite the gates to a large house, turn left onto a path that brings you to the canal bank. Now follow the bank until you meet with a bridge by Papercourt Lock.

2 Cross the bridge and continue left along the pretty towpath and pass the lock keeper's cottage. When a bridge over the canal is met, turn right and cross a smaller wooden bridge to a large meadow. Press on ahead on a distinct path and pass under power cables. At the bank of a small tributary of the River Wey, ignore a stile ahead of you and bear left along a farm track that eventually brings you to a road beside cottages.

3 Go rightwards alongside the road to soon meet a road junction. Now turn left along the A247 and cross the end of a road named Riverside Gardens. Press on ahead until the entrance drive to a large printing company is met. Here go left over a bridge and after 5 yards cross a stile on your right. Turn left now and follow the field edge as it runs parallel to the driveway. Maintain direction ahead at the end of the meadow and pass by a football pitch. The path now goes through a small oak wood and brings you to another meadow. Press on ahead to

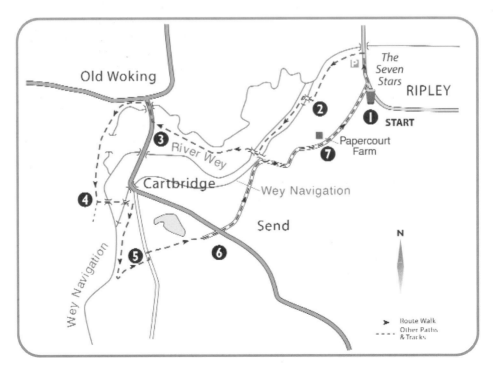

finally reach the entranceway to Fisher's Farm.

4 Turn left here and continue along a concrete drive to cross a bridge. After going over a second bridge bear right to meet up with the canal. Take the footbridge over the canal and follow the canal bank rightwards, where we soon pass a small lock called Worsfold Gates. Continue along the bank and turn left on an enclosed path 70 yards before meeting a bridge. This little path soon leads you between houses to meet a residential road.

5 Turn left and continue along the road for 40 yards and then turn right along another signposted path between houses. When another path joins it at the end of a large lake keep ahead to soon reach a quiet residential road by Hillside Farm. Go left along the road to pass a football pitch and meet a road junction.

6 Go ahead along Tannery Lane at this junction and continue on this fairly quiet lane as it takes you past what was the old tannery and finally brings you to Papercourt Farm.

7 The route continues along the lane until it ends beside the Seven Stars but as an alternative you could add an extra ½ mile to the route by going left here between the farmhouse and a barn on a track that brings you to Papercourt Lock. Here turn right along the canal bank and retrace your steps back to the Seven Stars

A timeless pastoral scene along the banks of the Wey Navigation

and the end of this very pleasant and easy walk.

Place of Interest

RHS Wisley Garden covers 240 acres and shows off British gardening at its very best. There are glasshouses with exotic plants, model gardens and extensive colourful planting throughout the year. Also on site are a restaurant, cafeteria, gift shop and large plant centre. It is signposted from the A3 two miles south-east of Ripley. Open March to October 10 am to 6 pm weekdays (9 am weekends) and November to February 10 am to 4.30 pm each day. Telephone: 01483 224234.

Date walk completed:

....

Burrowhill

The Four Horseshoes

This easy walk starts from alongside the village green which retains its pump and active smithy. After leaving Burrowhill behind, the route follows wide tracks across an area of Chobham Common called Albury Bottom. Later the way passes to the south of the indistinct remains of an ancient earthwork. At the halfway point the route climbs a low ridge, from where the views are far-reaching and panoramic. The sandy terrain is a haven for wildlife and birds and rare insects are plentiful.

The Four Horseshoes is a charming little pub set back from the road facing the small triangular village green. The cosy bars have beamed ceilings and a rural olde worlde village atmosphere. From the pumps come Courage Best, Bombardier and Brakspear's bitters while in the separate dining area there is a wide choice of scrumptious food.

Opening times are from 11 am to 3 pm and 5.30 pm to 11 pm (Sundays 12 noon to 3 pm and 7 pm to 10.30 pm) with food served between 12 noon and 2 pm and 7 pm to 9.30 pm each day. Booking is advisable.

Telephone: 01276 857581.

Distance: *3½ miles*

OS Explorer 160 Windsor, Weybridge and Bracknell
GR 970629

An easy walk on fairly level ground

Starting point: The Four Horseshoes car park. Please obtain permission to leave your car. Alternatively, park beside the village green

How to get there: Burrowhill is on the B383 and 1 mile north of the centre of Chobham.

The Walk

1 With the pub at your back, turn left and cross the B383 and continue along Gorse Lane. Soon pass the end of Heather Way and keep ahead along Gorse Lane. After rounding a bend and when beside Gorse Cottage you should bear left onto a public bridleway that continues alongside an electricity sub-station. After a few yards a large junction of tracks is met. Keep ahead here along the marked bridleway that soon runs alongside the heath with fields seen through the trees to your left. Ignore paths to left and right and keep ahead on the main track.

2 Eighty yards after passing under power cables a junction of paths is met. Here turn right along the wide ride. In 25 yards ignore a left turn and keep ahead. After 100 yards, at another junction of paths, go ahead along the left fork. Our way remains parallel to the line of power cables on your right and you should soon ignore a right fork. At the top of a low rise press on over a crossing track. Continue ahead over a second one and go up a low rise to meet a marker post by a third small crossing track.

3 Follow the path that sweeps away to your left. With the ride and line of power cables now behind you, continue along this well trodden path towards a low ridge ahead of you. Soon the path takes you to the top of the ridge. After the path levels out pass through a small stand of pine trees to meet a path on your left. Ignore this path unless you wish to take

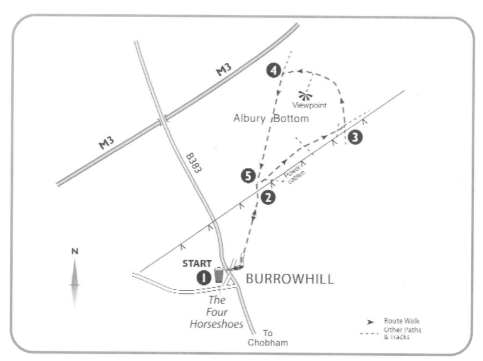

55

An expanse of heather at Albury Bottom

advantage of seats that offer panoramic views. After sampling these delights, return to the original route. Continuing ahead downhill we meet a junction of tracks after 40 yards. Ignore paths immediately on your right and bear half-right along the main path to soon pass a boarded walkway and in 10 yards meet a junction of tracks at the foot of the slope.

4 Turn hard left here along a wide straight ride where in the distance you will see the line of power cables. Now ignore any side paths and continue on this well used track until finally, when you are quite near the cables, you meet a T-junction.

5 Turn right here and after 25 yards turn left along a bridleway walked on the outward part of this walk. With the heath to your left and fields visible through the trees on your right, press on ahead to rejoin Gorse Lane. Continue along the road and soon the Four Horseshoes and the end of this short walk will be met.

Date walk completed:

....

Place of Interest
Brooklands Museum is sited off Brooklands Road, Weybridge, 5 miles east of Chobham. Old cars and aircraft plus picnic areas make this an interesting place to visit. Open Tuesday to Sunday all year plus Bank Holiday Mondays. Telephone: 01932 857381.

The Sun Inn

Although much of Dunsfold is now under the plough it retains the wildness of old Surrey. The hedgerows are filled with wild flowers during springtime and the air is alive with birdsong. This pretty route is across gently undulating farmland interspersed with pockets of woodland. For most of the way it follows little-used country lanes and farm tracks where the scenery is outstanding.

The Sun Inn is warmed by two log fires during winter while in the summer months tables are set out in the garden. The menu offers anything from spinach and mushroom lasagne with salad to Aberdeen Angus filleted steak. On my last visit I enjoyed a jacket potato dripping with melted cheese, washed down by good real ale.

Opening times are from 11 am to 11 pm each day (Sunday 12 noon to 10.30 pm) with cooked food served from 12 noon to 2.30 pm and 7 pm to 9.15 pm each day (sandwiches and baps throughout the day). Booking is advised during summer weekends.

Telephone: 01483 200242.

Distance: *5 miles*

OS Explorer 134 Crawley and Horsham GR 005363

An easy walk over gently undulating terrain

Starting point: The Sun Inn (park around the green by the pub).

How to get there: Dunsfold is signposted off the A281 at Nanhurst crossroads 6 miles south of Guildford. The Sun Inn is to the south end of the village.

The Walk

1 With the pub at your back turn right and right again and walk along Oak Tree Lane. At Mill Lane continue ahead along it to soon reach woodland. Press on ahead downhill through trees to reach and cross the tiny River Arun. Continue on a narrower path to reach the drive to Mill House.

2 Turn right and re-cross the river and then turn left immediately at the end of the bridge. Go through a gate and follow the riverbank and soon you will come upon an ancient well, whose waters are said to cure eye disorders. Cross a stile and turn rightwards uphill on a wide track to meet Dunsfold's treasure, the church of St Mary and All Saints. Built in

1260 it still has many of the original fittings, from the rare triple sedilia to the rough-hewn oak pews that are the oldest in Britain. The massive oak door and ironwork were made a century later, but something much older awaits outside by the porch - a thousand-year-old yew tree now looking its age. From the lychgate the route goes diagonally right along a small lane, which we follow to reach a T-junction with another. Turn left here and continue along the quiet lane to reach the driveway to Field Place.

3 Turn left and follow the drive across open fields with wonderful views. Just before meeting the house, you should bear leftwards on a farm track. This winding track brings you to the gates of Dunsley Farm. Continue past the

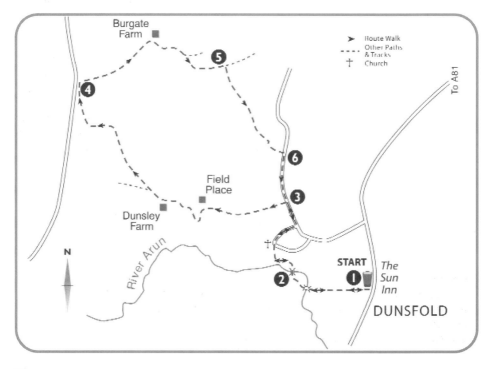

farmhouse and then bear right on a bridleway when beside a barn. Continue along the right-hand side of a field to reach a marker post after 120 yards. Here, leave the bridleway and turn right on a signposted footpath that crosses the centre of a field. At the far side cross a planked bridge over a stream and press on along the left side of another field. Pass through a gate and continue on a well-defined path that follows a stream through pretty woodland. Keep to the path as it crosses the stream and at the top of a small rise turn right by a fence. Exit the wood and keep ahead along the left side of a field and pass by a lovely garden and old house to reach a small road.

A 1,000-year-old yew stands by St Mary and All Saints church

❹ Go ahead to a fingerpost and take a bridleway rightwards along the drive to Burgate Farm. Keep to the drive as it bends right by the farm and soon ends by a large barn. Maintain direction ahead along a farm track and whilst still within sight of the barn bear right at a fork. When passing woodland on your right, look out for a signposted footpath also on the right.

❺ Follow this footpath through dense stands of pine alongside a field. Keep to the path as it kinks first left and then right when at the end of the field. At a field, cross a stile and go ahead along the right-hand edge. Cross two more stiles in quick succession and keep ahead along a field edge. Cross a stile to your right when beside a house and continue to the left along a driveway to soon reach a quiet country lane.

❻ Turn right along the lane and pass the drive to Field Place. Turn right at the next lane and retrace your steps back to the church. From here follow the downhill track to reach the River Arun and continue retracing your route to the Sun Inn and the end of this pretty walk.

> **Date walk completed:**
>
> ....

Place of Interest

Winkworth Arboretum is 4 miles north of Dunsfold off the B2130. Owned by the National Trust, the arboretum makes a lovely place to visit especially during spring and autumn when the colours are stunning. The hillside woodland with impressive azaleas and two peaceful lakes is open daily until dusk all year. Telephone: 01483 208477.

The White Horse

Writers often describe Shere as Surrey's jewel in the crown and how right they are. Picturesque narrow streets, old cottages, tea shops, a clear stream and a couple of great pubs; what more could you wish for in any village? The route begins in an eastward direction to reach Abinger Hammer. From here there is a climb of 350 ft to reach the top of the North Downs. The route returns to the valley floor on a fairly steep path and passes the Silent Pool, before rejoining the Tilling Bourne.

The White Horse is a lovely old pub which dates from the 15th century. It was reputedly a haunt of smugglers - Surrey, it seems, was overrun with them. Food is served all day every day from an ever-changing and comprehensive menu. Bookings are not taken so during the busy summer weekends it is first come first served. The pumps deliver Courage Best, Directors, Old Speckled Hen and a beer called Lock, Stock & Barrel.

Opening times are from 11 am until 11 pm each day (Sundays 12 noon until 10.30 pm).

Telephone: 01483 202518.

Distance: *7¼ miles*

OS Explorer 145 Guildford and Farnham GR 073477

A fairly easy walk with one long ascent and one steep descent, otherwise gently undulating

Starting point: The White Horse. There is no parking at the pub so park on street nearby, around the village or by the recreation ground in Upper Street.

How to get there: Shere is 6 miles west of Dorking and just off the A25.

The Walk

1 With the pub at your back go ahead along a lane and pass to the right of the war memorial. When alongside the church turn right through a gate on a rising path to reach a second gate. Turn left here and follow a well-trodden path as it runs alongside a line of oak trees. Keep to this well-defined path and soon after passing a block of garages you will meet a small drive. Continue leftwards along the drive to reach a road junction.

2 Continue ahead along High View and at a bend turn right and pass under a railway bridge. After 20 yards bear left onto a bridleway and soon pass to the left of a house on a narrow path that edges a field. At a quiet country lane, bear right along it and at a sharp right-hand bend go left onto a narrow bridleway. Soon it meets a driveway, which you now follow to meet the busy A25.

3 Turn right along the road for a short distance and enter Abinger Hammer. Now turn left up a small lane immediately before Abinger's clock. At the top of the incline ignore paths to left and right and press on ahead to reach a small group of cottages. Bear left at a fork to meet a railway. Stop, look and listen before crossing to the path opposite. Our route now follows an ancient track to the top of the downs. Ignore a signposted path on your right halfway up and continue ahead until you finally meet a junction of paths by open downland just below the crest of the hill.

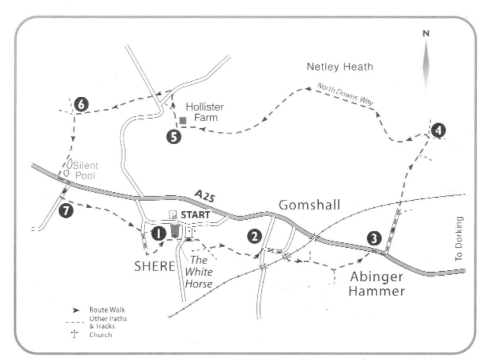

4 Turn left across Blatchford Down on the signposted North Downs Way long distance path. Within yards magnificent views over the Tilling Bourne valley open up before you. The more observant may notice orchids growing in the short grasses along here. Do be careful not to trample on or pick them. Now follow the NDW and acorn signs for 2 miles along a wide track through peaceful woodland until the stables of Hollister Farm are reached.

5 After passing the stables go right with the farm lane and soon, at a fork, keep ahead along the main track. At a second fork bear right along the North Downs Way to soon meet a road. Turn right along the road for 30 yards and then turn left along the NDW. Cross a road and press on through West Hanger car park to continue along the North Downs Way. Soon after going down a shallow slope a junction of tracks is met and it is here that we leave the long distance path.

6 Turn left at this junction of tracks on a path signposted to the Silent Pool. This downhill chalk path can become slippery after rain so take care. This path will bring you to a clear natural spring that feeds the Silent Pool and Sherbourne Pond. The circuit continues a few yards further to meet the A25. Cross the dual carriageway to the footpath opposite and go left alongside the road to meet a road junction. Turn right along this smaller road on a tarmac path that runs between a hedgerow and a fenced field. At the end of the field turn left onto a farm track.

7 The farm track soon ends at a stile, which you cross and keep ahead over a

Abinger Hammer, famous for its clock

meadow to another stile. Cross this and continue through woodland, at the end of which you cross another pretty meadow to reach a small country lane. Turn right along the lane and cross the Tilling Bourne beside a ford. Turn left through a kissing gate on a path that follows the stream. Go through a second kissing gate and continue along an unmade lane that brings you to the cottages of Shere. Press on and soon after passing the old prison you meet the centre of the village, the White Horse and the end of this lovely walk.

Place of Interest

Shere Museum is just a few yards south of the White Horse in a former maltings. The extensive displays of tools, toys and domestic items stretch from Victorian times to the 1950s. Open Easter to September on weekdays (except Wedesday) from 1 pm to 6 pm. Telephone: 01483 203245.

Date walk completed:

....

The Running Horse

Within yards of leaving the Running Horse the route follows the sparkling waters of the River Mole. It then passes by a small vineyard before reaching the extensive woodland of Norbury Park and on to the top of the Mole Gap. From here, there are panoramic views over the Mole Valley. The way then descends to meet up with the riverbank again, where we retrace our steps back to Leatherhead.

The **Running Horse** dates back to the 15th century and is Leatherhead's oldest pub. It offers a good selection of ales that will please all tastes. The choice of food is also splendid and ranges from sandwiches, toast melts, and fish dishes to more substantial meals such as traditional steak and kidney pudding. There is a pleasant garden and patio for those warmer summer days.

Opening times are from 11 am to 11 pm each day (Sunday 12 noon to 10.30 pm) with food being served from 12 noon to 3 pm and 6 pm to 10 pm daily (Sunday 12 noon to 6.30 pm).

Telephone: 01372 372081.

Distance: *4¾ miles*

OS Explorer 146 Dorking, Box Hill and Reigate
GR 164564

An easy walk over fairly level ground

Starting point: The Running Horse, where there is limited parking. There is a pay & display car park (free on Sundays) next door.

How to get there: Leatherhead is off junction 9 of the M25. The pub is in Bridge Street.

The Walk

1 With the pub behind you, turn right and cross the road bridge over the River Mole. Immediately after the bridge turn left on a narrow concrete path that soon brings you to a well-manicured meadow. Press on alongside the river until a tarmac drive is met. Turn right here along the drive and at a fork keep to the left. Soon after the drive has passed the buildings of Thorncroft Vineyard, it narrows and climbs up Hawk's Hill.

2 Cross a railway bridge and keep ahead over an open piece of grassland to meet posts at the far side. Now turn right along a rising chalk path to meet a T-junction. Turn left here along a bridleway that eventually brings you to a road.

Cross the road and follow a drive to the right to meet the entrance to Bockett's Farm. Press on ahead with a car park on your right and follow a well-trodden track beside fields. Ignore a woodland trail on your left and also a footpath a little later. Remain on the main path until a junction of tracks is met just yards after passing a brick-built byre.

3 Our way is to the left on a rising track through woodland, but should you wish to rest awhile there is a well placed seat just ahead of you under a spreading beech tree. This track is lined by spindle trees that are only conspicuous during autumn, when their brightly coloured fruits are displayed. Keep to a left fork as the track now crosses a wonderful wildflower meadow. At the far side of the meadow

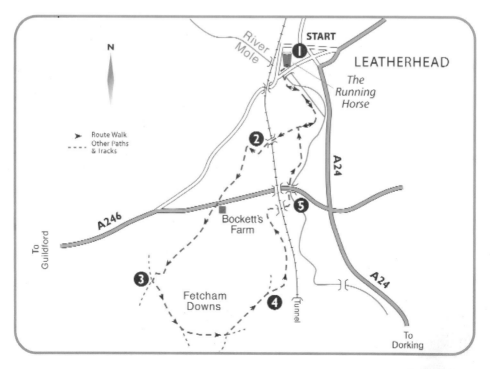

The sparkling waters of the River Mole near Leatherhead

press on ahead to meet up with a junction of tracks by picnic tables. Our way is through a gate to your left, signposted 'To the sculpture'. Follow this lovely path through peaceful woodland and pass the sculpture, which you will see to your left. Soon a track comes in from the right and we press on ahead. Not long after this, at a fork in the path, bear right to soon meet a stile at a field edge.

4 Cross the stile and bear diagonally leftwards to meet a stile in the bottom-left corner of this large field. Cross the stile and maintain direction along the right-hand edge of the next field. Go through a kissing gate, pass under a railway line and press on ahead, ignoring a second kissing gate to your right. Pass the end of a car park to meet up with the bank of the River Mole.

5 Turn left here and follow the path as it soon passes under a road bridge. The path gradually leaves the river to continue alongside the growing-grounds of Thorncroft Vineyard. As well as grapevines you will also notice rows of elderberry being cultivated. Go through a kissing gate to meet a junction of tracks ahead of you. Turn right here along the tarmac drive and just before it crosses the river, turn left along the riverbank and retrace your steps to Leatherhead.

Date walk completed:

....

Place of Interest

Polesdon Lacey, a beautiful country mansion built around 1820, contains many fine paintings and furniture and is 2½ miles west of Leatherhead off the A246. Open from March to early November, Wednesday to Sunday, 11 am until 5 pm. The gardens are open all year round from 11 am to 6 pm or dusk if earlier. Telephone: 01372 458203.

The Blue Ball

The circuit starts near Mere Pond, a small body of water that until 1898 was the village's only water supply. Following well-defined paths over the lovely expanse of Banstead Heath the route makes its way to the rim of Colley Hill. The views are spectacular. After leaving the hillside behind, the route passes along scenic paths as it crosses Walton Heath, radiant in spring with gorse and birch. For a while the path follows the edge of the celebrated golf course, where both royalty and the merely famous have played.

The Blue Ball is welcoming, comfortable, and functional. The choice of well-kept beers is good and includes Old Speckled Hen, Wadsworth 6X, Courage Best, Fullers London Pride and John Smith's Extra Smooth plus a choice of four lagers. Outside there is a popular sunny garden and patio.

Opening times are from 11 am to 11 pm (Sunday 12 noon to 10.30 pm) with food being served between 12 noon and 9.45 pm (Sunday 8.45 pm). It is advisable to book if wishing to order a meal at weekends.

Telephone: 01737 812168.

Distance: 5 miles

OS Explorer 146 Dorking, Box Hill and Reigate
GR 228553

An easy walk on level ground

Starting point: The Blue Ball car park. Please ask first about leaving your car, or park along the roadside.

How to get there: Walton-on-the-Hill is 1½ miles east of the A217 roundabout at Tadworth. The pub is to the right in Deans Lane opposite Mere Pond.

The Walk

1 With the pub at your back, cross the road and walk to a fingerpost ahead. Turn right along a bridleway and at a second post keep ahead on the bridleway signed to Dorking Road. At the road, cross with caution to the path opposite. Bear right along the bridleway signposted to Hogden Bottom. Soon, at a T-junction at the bottom of a slope, turn right and skirt the rear of a large garden.

2 After passing the garden you will meet another T-junction, where you should now turn left along a track signposted to Lower Kingswood. Maintain direction along this peaceful track until you meet a further junction of tracks by open downland. Go ahead, bearing slightly to the left, and continue along a path with a ribbon of trees close to your right.

3 Press on through trees to again find yourself facing open downland. Remain ahead on the bridleway signposted to Mogador and after 200 yards go through a gate. Now press on between fields to eventually reach a road. Bear right along the road and pass the Mint Arms, a fine Surrey watering hole.

4 Continue along the road, which soon develops into a cart track. Bear right into Margery Wood National Trust car park and pass an information board. Keep to the broad track through a bluebell wood, to pass over the M25. Pass through a gate and keep ahead to reach the open hillside and its magnificent views.

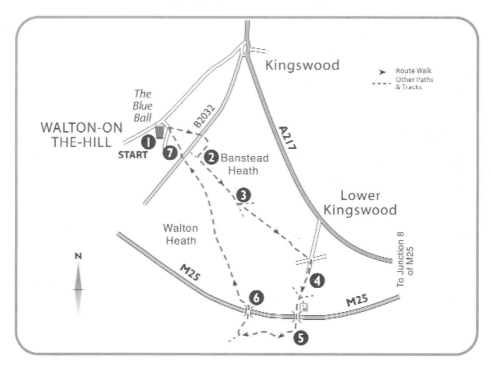

67

5 These lovely grassy slopes are under threat from the incursion of hawthorn, so cattle have been employed recently to help control the growth. The way lies to the right along the edge of the escarpment. When the open grassland ends, ignore a gate ahead of you and bear right to soon meet a track by another gate. Continue leftwards through the gate and continue between gardens. Ten yards after passing a coal duty post bear right at a fork and soon reach a quiet lane by a second duty post. Turn right along the lane and keep ahead to re-cross the M25.

The slopes of Colley Hill

6 Immediately after crossing the bridge turn left on a bridleway. The track now goes through lovely woodland and soon continues alongside Walton's famous golf course. At a junction of paths by yet another coal duty post press on ahead. When the open grassland of Banstead Heath is met, bear half left along a well-defined bridleway, again alongside the golf course. Later, ignore a right fork and remain alongside the golf course and before long you will find yourself at Dorking Road.

7 Cross to the driveway opposite and after 5 yards bear right on a narrow path. Keep to this path without deviation and before long you will see the Blue Ball pub to your right.

Place of Interest
The Bourne Hall Museum in Spring Street, Ewell, will transport you into the past. Some 5 miles north of Walton-on-the-Hill and just off the A24, this interesting place has exhibits ranging from a prime minister's hansom cab, an ancient fire engine and collections of old toys, cameras and costumes. There is also a cafeteria where you can enjoy a hot drink and light meals. Telephone: 020 8394 1734.

Date walk completed:

....

This super walk starts in the old wealden iron village of Charlwood. Soon it heads off through pretty Glover's Wood, where primroses line the banks of small brooks that carve their way deeply between the trees. These remnants of the ancient forest are thankfully preserved by The Woodland Trust, who encourage you to explore their beauty. The way then passes across scenic meadows offering far-reaching and magnificent views before making for the quiet hamlet of Cudworth.

The Rising Sun has built itself a reputation for good wholesome food. The popular restaurant has a varied and ever changing menu that majors on seafood. There are always vegetarian choices and children have their own options. During summer Sundays, weather permitting, a barbecue sizzles in the pretty rear garden.

Opening times are from 11 am to 11 pm each day (Sundays 10.30 pm) with cooked food available from 12 noon to 2.30 pm and 6 pm to 9 pm each day (Sunday 12 noon to 4 pm).

Telephone: 01293 862338.

Distance: *5¾ miles*

OS Explorer 146 Dorking, Box Hill and Reigate
GR 244401

An easy walk on fairly level ground

Starting point: The Rising Sun car park. Please obtain permission to leave your car, or park around the village.

How to get there: Charlwood is 3 miles west of the A217 at Horley. The pub is in the main street near the green.

The Walk

1 With the pub at your back, turn right and walk alongside the road and after 50 yards bear left along a narrow one-way street. Pass the Half Moon pub and keep ahead on a path through the graveyard of St Nicholas's church. Exit the graveyard and continue on the path to soon reach a road junction. Go ahead along Glovers Road and when it ends at a gateway keep ahead on a signposted path and pass between buildings.

2 Continue ahead on a fenced path between fields and enter Glover's Wood. Keep to the signposted path and ignore nature trails to left and right.

3 As you exit woodland, cross a stile ahead and follow a signposted footpath between fields to meet a road. Here turn right along the road for 10 yards and then left on a fenced footpath beside a house. Cross a stile and press on ahead over a large field. With a small stream running along the bottom of a gully on your left, look out for a farm track that soon crosses it. Here go left to enter a second field and then turn immediately right and follow the field edge with the gully now to your right. At the corner of the field, bear right and then follow the gully left to meet a substantial wooden bridge, which you should cross to meet a stile at a field edge.

4 Cross the stile and bear left along a field edge to meet another stile. Cross this and pass through more woodland and

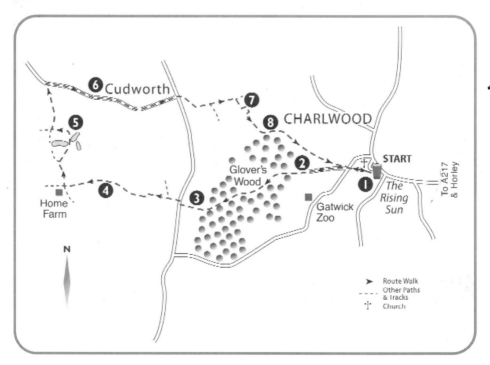

another two wooden bridges to meet a field. Go ahead across the centre of this and a second field to reach the buildings of Home Farm. At the farm drive, turn immediately right and after 8 yards, go through a metal gate. Pass by low farm buildings and continue through a second metal gate. Press on along the well-defined bridleway and cross a stile 8 yards to the right of a third metal gate. Now go diagonally right over a field to meet and cross a wooden bridge between two fishing lakes.

5 Maintain direction along a farm track and keep to it until it reaches a T-junction with another. Ignore a footpath ahead of you and turn right along a farm track; you soon pass through a gate and between farm buildings. Follow this pleasant track until it meets a small road junction. Here turn right along a country lane.

6 When you reach the interesting moated manor house at Cudworth, look out for its unusual roofed bridge that incorporates a built-in dovecote. Press on along the lane and ignore a right turn beside the old tithe barn. At a road junction, cross the stile ahead of you and bear diagonally right over a field to meet and cross a stile in the far right-hand corner. Keep ahead now along a right-hand field edge. Cross another stile and soon a stream in woodland. Turn right over a further stile to meet a well-worn path.

7 Ignore the path ahead of you and turn left along the well-trodden path. After

passing farm buildings look out for a stile on your right. Cross this and aim for the centre of two houses, where you cross a hidden stile. Go left for 30 yards then turn right along a field edge beside a house. Skirt a garden and continue along the field edge, ignoring a stile soon on your right. Press on down a gentle slope to re-join Glover's Wood.

8 Here follow a well-defined path leftwards that follows the woodland edge. When a stile by a field edge is met, go right alongside the field and soon ignore a farm track on your right. At the end of the field cross a stile and pass through a strip of woodland to meet and cross another stile. Now go ahead on the dip slope of the field to meet and cross a stile in the far corner. Press on to soon re-join Glovers Road, where you turn left and retrace your steps back to the Rising Sun.

Place of Interest

Gatwick Zoo is located in Rectory Lane, 1 mile north west of the centre of Charlwood, and is well signposted. There is also a coffee shop, gift shop and picnic areas. Open daily March to October from 10.30 am until 6 pm, and November to February from 10.30 am to 4 pm. Telephone: 01293 862313.

Date walk completed:

....

The Bell Inn

Within yards of the start, the way passes by Outwood's famous windmill, built in the plague year of 1665. The outward leg of the circuit follows field paths through farmland elevated enough to give striking views across the Surrey Weald. After

Distance: 5¼ miles

OS Explorer 146 Dorking, Box Hill and Reigate
GR 328456

An easy walk on fairly level ground

Starting point: The Bell Inn. Please obtain permission to leave your car, or use the National Trust car park 200 yards away.

How to get there: From the A25 at Bletchingley travel south for 3 miles along Outwood Lane. The pub is just before the windmill.

passing the ancient moat of Burstow Lodge the route continues along more field paths to reach the outskirts of Smallfield. Later, a lovely old byway that climbs slowly along a ribbon of woodland brings you back to Outwood.

The Bell Inn has been described as a 'diner's paradise'. There is a wide choice of food that includes breaded garlic mussels, spicy grilled swordfish and beef 'Bell'ington. The beers are well kept and include Harvey's Best and Young's Bitter plus guest ales.

Opening times are 11 am to 11 pm each day (Sunday 12 noon to 10.30 pm) with food served from 12 noon to 2 pm and 6.30 pm to 9.30 pm (Sunday 12 noon to 10.30 pm). Booking is essential during summer weekends and bank holidays.

Telephone: 01342 842989.

The Walk

1 With the pub behind you turn left to arrive at Outwood Common. Continue ahead and turn right into Millers Lane. Press on along the road and at a junction keep to the left fork. Soon after rounding a left-hand bend in the road turn left on a signposted footpath opposite Wasp Green Lane.

2 Go over a stile to another by a plank over a ditch. Cross the stile and go left along the field edge for 30 yards and then re-cross the ditch via a stile on your left. Turn right along the hedgerow and maintain direction ahead over another stile. Press on through a field gate and ignore a footpath to your left but cross a stile 50 yards ahead.

3 Keep ahead for 50 yards and then turn right along the top edge of a field with a line of oak trees immediately to your right and power cable to your left. Ignore a stile to your right and maintain direction to one ahead of you. Cross this and turn leftwards to cross a stile signed 'Tandridge Border Path'. Now bear right and continue downhill to a stile on the woodland edge. Pass through dappled woodland to reach a kissing gate, where you continue along a fenced path. Keep ahead over a further four stiles to reach a road.

4 Turn left along the road and after 80 yards turn right along a bridleway. At a farm track turn left and keep to it as it passes farm buildings. Ignore a drive to the right and pass between Bakers

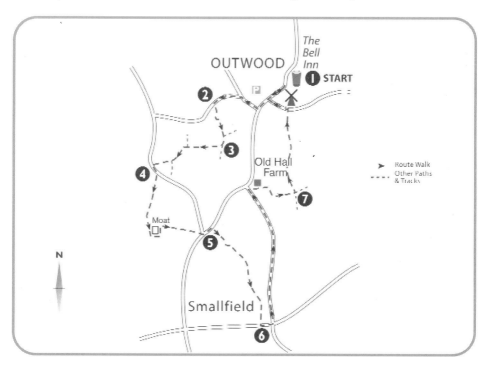

Farmhouse and the large barn of Burstow Manor. Follow the drive rightwards and stay on it until a road junction is reached.

5 Go ahead here along the road signed to Outwood and soon, at a bend, turn right onto a footpath along the driveway to Hollesley Farm. At the end of a pretty pond turn right alongside a large barn. At the end of the barn turn left for 5 yards and then right along an enclosed farm track. Soon, at a waymarked post, bear right on a narrow path to meet a stile. Continue through fields and over stiles as directed by the signs until soon after crossing a small stream a road is met.

6 Turn left along the road and very soon turn left again into Cogmans Lane, where you pass the entranceway of Smallfield Place. Keep to this pretty little lane until just before a road junction. The route now goes right over a stile to the left of a farm gate. Keep to the farm track as it winds between farm buildings. Soon the track bends to the right and ends at a field gate. Turn left here and continue along a well-defined footpath until it meets a rough track.

7 Turn left along the track and pass a cottage. Our way continues along this very pleasant byway until it finally ends beside a house named Knowle Green. Turn left along the road and within yards you pass the windmill. A few yards further to your right you will find the Bell Inn and the end of the walk.

Outwood windmill, built in 1665, is in perfect working order

Place of Interest

Outwood Windmill is open to the public every Sunday and bank holiday from Easter to September between the hours of 2 pm and 6 pm. There is a small museum in the cowshed and ducks, geese, sheep and goats run free in the grounds. Small children have their own play area.
Telephone: 01342 843458.

Date walk completed:

....

The Hare and Hounds

Early on in this excellent walk, you pass by the side of Bay Pond, a Surrey Wildlife Trust nature reserve. Soon the circuit meets the Greensand Way long distance path and follows it eastwards over arable fields with fine views. After passing through the hamlet of Tandridge, the route heads off to rejoin the Greensand Way just below Tilburstow Hill. A very pretty downhill path through the rolling countryside of Garston Park then brings us back to Godstone's village green.

The Hare and Hounds is a former brew house. The extensive menu of freshly cooked food runs from sandwiches and ploughman's lunches to main courses that include a seafood tagliatelle Provençal. Look out for the well-chosen specials posted daily on the blackboard. Quench your thirst on ales that include Fuller's London Pride, Young's Special and Harvey's Sussex Ale plus four different lagers.

Opening times are 11 am to 11 pm each day (12 noon to 10.30 pm Sundays) with food served at lunchtimes and evenings.

Telephone: 01883 742296.

Distance: *6 miles*

OS Explorer 146 Dorking, Box Hill and Reigate
GR 349516

An easy walk over undulating terrain

Starting point: The Hare and Hounds car park where there is limited parking (please ask first). Alternatively, use the small car park by the village pond.

How to get there: Godstone is just south of junction 6 of the M25.

The Walk

1 With the pub at your back go left to meet the road. Here, cross to a small lane opposite that soon meets the High Street. Cross the road and continue rightwards along the pavement and pass the village post office. Immediately after passing the White Horse, turn left along a small lane. Pass the village hall and continue along a tarmac path that takes you past Bay Pond to meet a road by the church of St Nicholas.

2 Turn right along the road and pass some very nice almshouses. Continue along this quiet lane to pass by a couple of old houses, the largest and finest being the Old Pack House. Continue on the lane until it ends at a T-junction. Now turn left along the road and at a bend bear left onto a bridleway signposted along a driveway. Soon, ignore a footpath to your left and continue along the drive, and over a small ford. After 10 yards bear right along the Greensand Way long distance path. At a fork keep ahead alongside a fence and at the crest of a rise ignore a path to your left and go ahead to meet a road.

3 Cross to the path opposite and maintain direction ahead over undulating fields to eventually meet another road in Tandridge. Turn right alongside the road and pass the Barley Mow, a fine Surrey watering hole. After passing the village school, continue alongside the road and

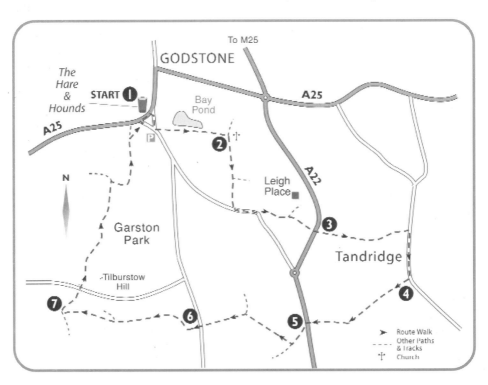

leave the hamlet behind. Look out for a signposted path to your right at a bend in the road by a speed restriction sign.

4 Cross a stile here and press on ahead alongside a hedgerow to go over a second stile in the bottom corner of the field. Cross a small bridge over a brook and bear diagonally left to meet and cross a stile. Now continue ahead along the right-hand field edge. Cross a further stile in the top corner of the field and turn left along the field edge for a few yards before turning rightwards alongside a fence. Keep ahead now to reach a stile at the top of the field. Cross this and now bear right down a sloping field and go through a gap in the hedgerow ahead of you. Pass along a line of oak trees to meet a road.

5 Turn left alongside the road for a few yards before turning right over a stile. Now go diagonally left across a field to a corner of a coppice. Cross a stile on your right and cross the centre of the next field to meet a marker post by trees. Pass this and bear diagonally right to the top of the field to meet and cross a stile. Turn left now along a path that forms a part of the Greensand Way to eventually meet a road.

6 Cross the road diagonally rightwards and continue along the signposted broad Greensand Way path. After ¾ mile the Greensand Way kinks to the right by a

The Old Pack House

gate and a stile. Here, go ahead and cross the stile and press on along a field edge to eventually meet a lane.

7 Turn right along the rising lane to meet a road junction. Go ahead to the path opposite and follow this as it leads you through Garston Park. At a driveway maintain direction ahead and then, 30 yards after passing a barn, bear left along the drive. When a road is reached turn right along it to meet up with Godstone's village green. Turn right alongside the green to the duck pond and by following the road leftwards you will soon be back at the Hare and Hounds and the end of this walk.

Date walk completed:

....

Place of Interest
Godstone Farm is just south of the village in Tilburstow Hill Road. The children's farm is in a lovely setting with lots of things to do and see: cuddly animals, good play equipment, large sandpits and an indoor play barn. Open all year from 10 am until 6 pm (5 pm during winter). Telephone: 01883 742546.

The Plough Inn

This is a good walk for any time of year except for 24th March of each year, when the parkland is closed. Our way is along tarmac driveways, farm tracks and easy-to-follow bridleways, making it ideal for the whole family. We follow the long and delightful driveway of Greathed Manor, where there are pretty views across the well-kept parkland. The route continues through oak woodland where, almost unnoticed, it gains 200 ft in height. Soon the way turns northward and follows a bridleway through attractive woodland before returning to the start.

The Plough Inn is the perfect place for refreshment. From the pumps come Greene King IPA, London Pride, Adnams and Brakspear's bitters as well as the usual offerings of wine, lager and stout. The scrumptious food is home cooked to order, so you may have to wait a bit, but it is worth it! As well as a good choice of starters, the main course selections cover anything from fish and chips and brie and broccoli en croute to T-bone grills.

Opening times are 11 am to 11 pm each day (Sunday 12 noon to 10.30 pm).

Telephone: 01342 832933.

Distance: *4 miles*

OS Explorer 147 Sevenoaks and Tonbridge GR 406428

An easy walk on fairly level ground

Starting point: The Plough Inn car park. Please ask first about leaving your car; alternatively, park alongside verges.

How to get there: From Lingfield travel east along the B2028. Pass under a railway bridge and the Plough Inn will be met at the second junction on your right.

The Walk

1 With the pub behind you, go right and then right again into Ford Manor Road past charming old cottages. At a fork in the lane bear right and continue along the tarmac drive to Greathed Manor. The drive offers pleasing views across parkland towards the North Downs. At a junction of paths near a cottage, keep ahead along the drive.

2 Twenty yards after passing the entrance to the manor house bear right on a drive, to pass by a house and stabling. Keep ahead along a farm track until, soon after crossing a small stream, the track bears off to the left. Leave the track here and maintain direction ahead between posts. Now continue on a smaller track that climbs easily through oak woodland and at the top of the rise go between farm buildings to meet a tarmac drive.

3 Turn left along this quiet driveway, which now offers panoramic views over the adjoining countryside. Pass Old Lodge Farm and maintain direction when a small group of cottages is met.

4 Turn left on a signposted bridleway immediately after passing the last cottage. This narrow path first zig-zags alongside meadows before leading you through pretty woodland. After exiting the trees the path continues between fields, with more scenic views, to end at a T-junction.

5 Our circuit continues leftwards along

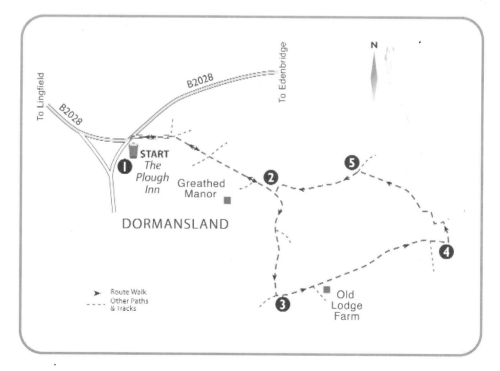

The delightful countryside around Dormansland

a farm track to pass Littleworth Cottage. When the farm track ends by a gate, go ahead through the gate and press on through lovely woodland. After leaving the woodland continue along an unmade driveway, to pass a house and farm buildings. Soon after rounding a bend, turn right alongside a barn to rejoin the original outward route. Press on along the Greathed Manor driveway now to meet Ford Manor Road leading to the delights of the Plough Inn.

Date walk completed:

....

Place of Interest
Greathed Manor has variously been described as having an exterior that is 'a fine example of Victorian architecture' and 'architecture that bears no coherent style'. The interior is worth seeing, though, with impressive wood panelling and ornately moulded ceilings. The manor house is open from Easter until September on Wednesdays and Thursdays from 2 pm until 4 pm. Telephone: 01342 832577.

The Anchor Bleu

This short but interesting walk starts near the water's edge in the picturesque old village of Bosham. The route heads inland and continues eastwards through level fields. With super views over to the South Downs, it then turns south for a short distance before heading west over more open country. As the circuit nears Bosham it meets the water's edge and passes along the appealing foreshore.

The Anchor Bleu is a lovely little pub dating back over 300 years and its setting on the waterfront makes it a very popular spot with visitors. There is a tiny garden to the front and a smaller patio overlooking the sea at the rear. As well as a good choice of beers, the pub offers a reasonable choice of food with daily 'specials' on offer, as well as bar snacks such as ploughman's or soup and a roll.

Opening times are 11 am to 11 pm daily (Sunday, 12 noon to 10.30 pm). The daily 'specials' menu is available from 12 noon to 2 pm, bar snacks from 2 pm to 6 pm and a further bar menu from 7 pm to 9 pm. Bookings are not taken.

Telephone: 01243 573956.

Distance: *3 miles*

OS Explorer 120 Chichester
GR 805039

An easy walk, on level ground

Starting point: The pay & display car park near the foreshore in Bosham.

How to get there: Bosham is signposted from the A27 south of Chichester. Follow the signs to Bosham church and quay.

The Walk

① If you wish to visit the Anchor Bleu before your walk, turn left and in a few yards turn right along a narrow lane to soon find the pub. To start the circuit, turn right out of the vehicular entrance of the car park and walk along the main street, heading away from the water's edge. Keep to the village street to eventually pass the Berkeley Arms.

② Ignore a left turn here and continue ahead until the road finally bends to the left besides the entrance to Rectory Farm. Leave the road now and continue ahead on a well-trodden path that leads you over fields. After passing a very large commercial growing area to your left, a wide crossing track is met. Keep ahead here and after 150 yards turn right onto a signposted footpath along a field edge to soon meet a quiet country lane.

③ Maintain direction ahead along the lane which offers fine views across the fields to the South Downs. If you are as lucky as I was when last passing this way, you may be treated to the sight of kestrels hunting in the surrounding fields.

④ On a left bend in the lane, turn right onto a signposted fenced path. After going between level fields, the path leads you past an isolated house and, for a short distance, along its driveway. When the drive bends sharply left, turn right onto a signposted path and in a few yards

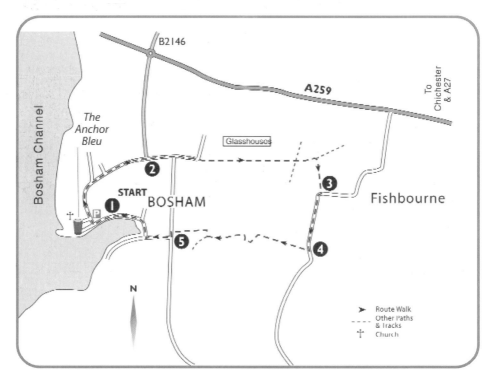

The foreshore at Bosham

turn left across the middle of a field to soon reach a road by a flint cottage named Byways.

5 Turn left along the road and then right into Stumps Lane. Soon you will see the channel inlet ahead of you, with the houses of Bosham fronting the water and the church steeple beyond. Turn right into Shore Road and, just yards after passing the old National School, bear left. The road is flooded at each tide so, depending on the tide, either follow the raised path or the foreshore road back to Bosham and the start of the walk.

Place of Interest

Fishbourne Roman Palace, in Salthill Road, Fishbourne lies 1½ miles east of Bosham and is signposted from the A259. These are the remains of the largest Roman residence known in Britain. There are beautiful mosaics, a museum, gardens and a Roman gardening museum. Telephone: 01243 785859.

Date walk completed:

....

The White Horse Inn

Chilgrove, a small hamlet consisting of not much more than a few scattered farms and half a dozen houses, is the starting point for this lovely walk. The route is along wide paths, cart tracks and quiet country lanes that make it so easy to follow. Starting off westerly along a woodland path, it soon passes through Hooksway, where a slow climb brings you to the very top of the downs some 500 ft above Chilgrove. After following the top of the downs for almost a mile, the route turns south through Westdean Woods. The pretty path is on a gentle downhill slope and leads you through extensive pine forest where the glorious scent of pine fills the air. At the valley floor the way follows a little used country lane, which takes you back to the White Horse Inn.

The White Horse Inn is an independently owned and very popular inn. It is a blend of traditional village pub, quality restaurant and luxury hotel. Serving anything from an Italian-style open sandwich in the bar to a wild rabbit casserole with Muscat wine and grape sauce in the restaurant, the owner's team of French chefs certainly excel.

Opening hours are 12 noon to 3 pm and 6 pm to 11 pm each day with booking necessary at weekends if wishing to eat in the restaurant.

Telephone: 01243 535219.

Distance: *7¼ miles*

OS Explorer 120 Chichester
GR 828144

An easy walk, with one long uphill stretch

Starting point: The car park of the White Horse Inn. Please seek permission from the landlord to leave your car whilst you walk. Alternatively, you could park in the lane outside.

How to get there: Chilgrove is on the B2141, 7 miles north-west of Chichester.

The Walk

1 With the pub at your back, turn left and walk up the rising lane to a small road junction. Bear left here and after 100 yards go left onto a signposted footpath along a pleasant cart track.

2 The track will bring you to a stile at a field edge. Continue ahead over the field and pass under power cables. Continue through a coppice to a second field and cross this to the far left corner. Now go along a cart track through peaceful woodland and over two crossing tracks to finally meet a T-junction with a wide track. Turn right along the track and soon ignore a stile to your left. The track ends at the Royal Oak pub in Hooksway.

3 Now turn right along the road for a short distance and 10 yards after passing a small building to your left, you will find a junction of paths and tracks. Ignore the footpath to the right and also the bridleway that forks to the left. Our way is dead ahead on a signposted public right of way along a broad, stony, uphill track. Ignore side paths and remain ahead on this wide track until you eventually reach the top of Didling Hill.

4 Continue ahead along the fenced path that follows the top of the ridge and ignore the occasional path to the left. Soon after passing below the top of Linch Down and its trig point, you should look out for a waymarked path on your right.

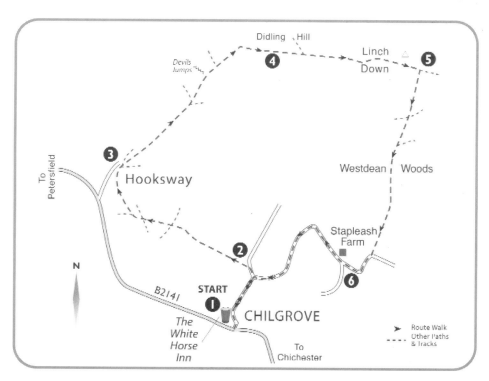

The path over Linch Down has fantastic views

5 Go right onto this path, alongside a line of beech trees, with a field to your left. This marvellous path will now lead you easily downhill through the majestic pines of Westdean Woods. Ignore any side paths and remain ahead at all times along the well-defined track on which you will pass strange, large, carved balls of chalk. Later, the track takes you alongside a Sussex Wildlife Trust nature reserve, passing by its hedge-layered boundary. Members of the Trust look after this beautiful place and practise the arts of coppicing and hedge-layering as well as preserving our flora and fauna. Eventually, you will be confronted by a gate across the track. Press on through this and then another to meet a quiet country lane.

6 Turn right along this lane and soon at a T-junction continue to the right and pass Staple Ash Farm. Keep to this small lane as it winds along the valley floor. After passing under power cables a road junction is met where you should now turn left and continue downhill, retracing your earlier steps to the White Horse Inn and all that it offers.

Date walk completed:

....

Place of Interest
Uppark is a fine late 17th-century house set on the South Downs and owned by the National Trust. The interior contains fine paintings, furniture and ceramics. The house is open from the end of March to the end of October between 1 pm and 5 pm Sunday to Thursday (last admission 4.15 pm). It is sited 4 miles west of Chilgrove and signposted from the B2141. Telephone: 01730 825857.

The Noah's Ark

This appealing and easy to follow circuit starts at one of the prettiest village greens in England. The route leads you through woods which, during spring, are carpeted in bluebells and are quite breathtaking. Before long the way meets the foot of Black Down Hill, which it skirts westwards. As the route turns south and crosses the elevated parkland of Blackdown Park the panoramic views are far-reaching and quite outstanding.

The Noah's Ark, built back in the mists of time, has a long history of brewing and baking. Privately owned and run, this welcoming village inn makes the perfect place to stop awhile. The bar snack and main course menus are full of mouth-watering selections, whether it is a sandwich you require or something more substantial.

Opening hours are 11 am to 3 pm and 6 pm to 11 pm each day (12 noon to 4 pm and 7 pm to 10.30 pm on Sundays). Booking at weekends is essential for cooked food.

Telephone: 01428 707346.

Distance: *4½ miles*

OS Explorer 133 Haslemere & Petersfield GR 937273

A fairly easy walk over hills.

Starting point: The village green in Lurgashall.

How to get there: Lurgashall is 5 miles north of Petworth and signposted off the A283. There is parking at the village green.

The Walk

1 With the pub behind you, turn right alongside the village green. Soon after the end of the green, turn right over a stile beside a house. Now follow this pleasant path through a couple of small orchards and paddocks. At woodland, press on ahead along the well-trodden path. In spring, these woods are full of bluebells.

2 When a wide farm track is met, fork rightwards and cross a stile marked with a yellow arrow. Continue ahead alongside the left edge of the field and cross a stile on the far side. Now go diagonally left along the next field edge to meet a marker post in 120 yards. Turn left here and in 20 yards, by a second marker post, go right and cross the centre of the field towards a house ahead of you. Cross a small-planked bridge, go through a gate and press on ahead through the garden to soon meet a gravel drive and a road beyond.

3 Turn right along this quiet road and pass the end of Quell Lane. After going through a dip, a road junction is met by a telephone box. Turn left here along the lane signposted to Roundhurst. Look out for a narrow bridleway on your left just after passing a house and barn. Take this bridleway which turns sharply back on itself and passes the rear of the house and barn. The path now climbs steadily along

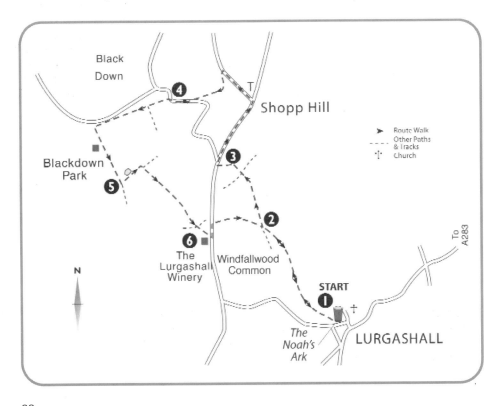

88

a ribbon of trees and offers fine views. Keep on it until a lane is met. Turn right and go uphill for a short distance.

4 Fork left on a path at a right bend in the road. Continue through woodland and at a drive press on ahead to meet a road. Maintain direction along the road and on a dip by a bend, turn left on a signposted footpath along the driveway to Blackdown Park. After 100 yards fork right by a directional post and leave the driveway. Cross an open piece of grass and, at a second post, cross the drive and keep ahead enjoying some of the best views Sussex has to offer. Continue through a gate and press on downhill on a fenced path to meet a stile on your left.

5 Go over the stile and ignore a path on your right. Now continue ahead along a farm track that soon passes a picturesque pond in a beautiful garden. At a barn, continue to the right along the farm track. Ignore a path over a cattle grid in 30 yards and continue on the broad downhill track to pass a lodge gatehouse. Ignore paths to left and right and keep ahead to soon reach a quiet lane beside the Lurgashall Winery.

6 The circuit continues leftwards along the lane for 120 yards before turning right along a farm drive. As you near

The Lurgashall Winery is passed along the way and makes an interesting place to stop

farm buildings at the end of the drive, fork left on a path that within yards brings you to a farm track. Go ahead here to soon meet a junction of paths alongside the stile you crossed on your outward journey. Fork left here and retrace your steps through the bluebell wood to reach the small paddocks and orchards. Soon reach the road where, by turning left, you will find the Noah's Ark and the end of this lovely walk.

Date walk completed:

....

Place of Interest

Lurgashall Winery in Dial Green, just ½ mile west of Lurgashall, is housed in a complex of old converted barns dating back to the 17th century. It makes an interesting place to visit. Try before you buy at the well-stocked wine shop that is open each day from 9 am to 5 pm (Sundays 11 am to 5 pm). Telephone: 01428 707292.

The Cricketers

This marvellous walk takes you across pretty rolling countryside below the South Downs where the views are far-reaching and outstanding. The route starts by crossing Burton Park before heading south for fine views across a peaceful vale towards the small hamlet of Sutton. Now the way turns westwards to reach Barlavington. After leaving this quiet place, more panoramic views are enjoyed before returning to Duncton.

The Cricketers is an award-winning pub, boasting a good restaurant. It serves an excellent and plentiful choice of food while the bar itself has a good choice of well-kept beers.

Opening hours are 11 am to 2.30 pm and 6 pm to 11 pm Monday to Friday, 11 am to 3 pm and 6 pm to 11 pm on Saturday; and 12 noon to 3 pm only on Sunday during winter. It is necessary to book a table if wishing to eat a cooked meal here at weekends.

Telephone: 01798 342473.

Distance: *6¼ miles*

OS Explorer 121 Arundel and Pulborough GR 960169

An easy walk over undulating terrain

Starting point: The Cricketers - please seek the landlord's permission before leaving your car whilst you walk. Alternatively, park on the road.

How to get there: The Cricketers sits on the A285, 4 miles south of Petworth.

The Walk

1 With the pub at your back, turn right and walk alongside the A285. Ignore a lane on your right after a few yards but turn right 10 yards after passing a bus stop onto a signposted footpath along a driveway. When the drive exits woodland by a gateway, bear left over a stile and continue over a grassy area to a small chapel where you rejoin the drive. Maintain direction along the drive between fields and follow it rightwards at a corner by an ancient chestnut tree with a huge girth.

2 The drive finally brings you to what can best be described as a small village green. Here you should continue ahead on a broad bridleway to pass a peaceful lake. Keep right at a fork and after going between banks, cross two stiles in quick succession to pass a cottage and meet a lane. Go ahead along the lane for 150 yards.

3 Turn right onto a bridleway beside a nature reserve. Keep alongside the fenced reserve as the path leads you through pretty woodland. Eventually keep ahead along a drive to meet a road. Turn right along the road and pass a large house called The Old Poor House. At the top of a rise, turn left along a farm track and follow it as it zigzags past the farmhouse and between fields. Soon, with a field gate to your left, you should leave the track and turn right on a sandy bridleway that takes you through the woodland.

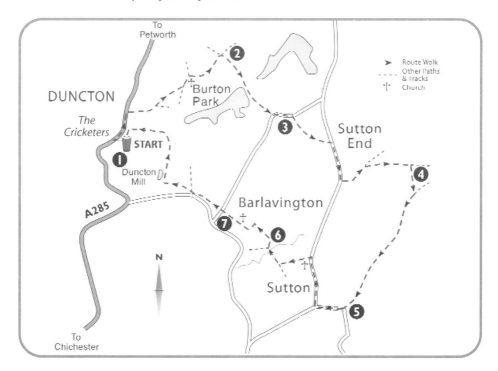

4 Turn right by a marker post on a slight downward slope and continue through a hazel coppice. Soon, ignore a left fork and press on ahead to meet a T-junction. Turn right here and ignore the occasional path to left and right. Keep to this straight path now until it meets a driveway. Continue along the drive to reach a road.

5 Go ahead along the road now and at the top of a rise you will come to a small road junction by the White Horse pub in Sutton. Turn right along the road and continue through this quiet little hamlet. Pass the village church and after 80 yards, turn left onto a drive. At the end of the drive continue ahead on a narrow downhill path through woodland. When the path ends at a T-junction with another, turn right on the downhill path. As you enter a ribbon of woodland ignore a stile on your right and press on to cross a stream and a stile ahead of you.

6 Ignore a path to your left and continue on a path that soon bears right to meet a stile in the top corner of the field. Cross this and turn left along a rising field edge until you reach a farm track by large barns. Turn left along the track and soon turn left again on a path through the graveyard of the picturesque 13th-century church in Barlavington. Exit the graveyard and turn left along a lane for 100 yards to meet a bend, where you

The route passes by the millpond and picturesque buildings of Duncton Mill

should now go ahead along a farm track in front of you to meet and pass through a gate.

7 Continue on an enclosed path that goes downhill to cross a stream and meet a lane. Press on up a stepped path opposite and continue through a field to finally meet and cross a stile at a road. Now bear immediately rightwards along a farm track. At the end of a field ignore a right turn and carry on ahead through woodland to reach a private driveway. The route continues rightwards along the drive where you soon pass the buildings of Duncton Mill. Follow this lane now to finally reach the A285, and turn left to meet the Cricketers pub within yards.

Date walk completed:

....

Place of Interest
Bignor Roman Villa is 3 miles east of Duncton on a well signposted minor road. The site contains one of the largest Roman villas found in Great Britain. The beautifully preserved mosaic floors are on display during March and April Tuesday to Sunday from 10 am to 5 pm and from May to October daily between 10 am and 5 pm. Telephone: 01798 869259.

The Black Horse

Spectacular is the word to describe this walk on the South Downs which starts from the rose-bowered village of Amberley. The route begins by climbing Rackham Hill some 500 ft above the village. Although sounding a little extreme, the climb is not that difficult and, once at the summit, you can rest assured that from here the route is either gently downhill or level for its remainder. You will appreciate climbing to these heady heights for the magnificent uninterrupted panoramas to be seen over the countryside.

The Black Horse is a charming village pub that has more to offer than its exterior suggests. Flagstoned floors, old world charm and a good 70-seat restaurant. The choice of food is excellent and is cooked to order from the extensive menu, which includes items for children.

Opening hours are 11 am to 11 pm each day (Sundays 12 noon to 10.30 pm) with food served from 12 noon to 2.30 pm and 6.30 pm to 9.30 pm weekdays and 12 noon until 9 pm on weekends. Booking for the restaurant is essential.

Telephone: 01798 831552.

Distance: *8 miles*

OS Explorer 120 Chichester
GR 031133

An easy walk, apart from one long, steep climb

Starting point: The road in front of the Black Horse.

How to get there: From the large roundabout on the A29 north of Arundel, take the B2139, signposted to Amberley. Half a mile after crossing the River Arun, turn left into the village. The pub is at the end of the road.

93

The Walk

1 With the Black Horse at your back, turn left and walk along the road to the B2139. Here cross into Mill Lane, where the climb begins.

2 At a road junction, press on leftwards on the lane and then soon turn left on a stony track signposted 'South Downs Way'. The route follows the long distance footpath as it climbs to the top of the downs. After reaching Amberley Mount, the path eases and, without too much of a further rise, passes by the trig point on Rackham Hill. With the climb now over, continue ahead until, a few yards before a line of trees, a farm track joins the path from the right.

3 Here the circuit leaves the long distance path by turning sharply right along this track which leads you gently downhill through open fields with far-reaching views and you should keep to it until it forks.

4 Take the right-hand fork and remain on the farm track until it is joined by another at a gate. Maintain direction ahead and pass derelict farm buildings. The route continues downhill with views over the River Arun where it is possible to see the ramparts of Arundel Castle beyond. Finally, you arrive at the small hamlet of North Stoke.

5 Turn right at a small road junction and continue around an S-bend. Some 10

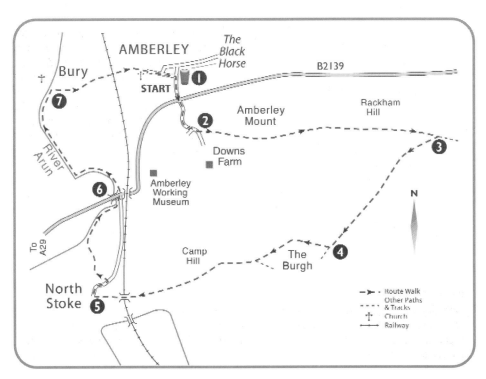

Picturesque thatched cottages line the village street in Amberley

yards after passing a row of half-tile hung cottages turn left through a gate. Follow this enclosed path until you meet the bank of the River Arun. Turn right here and walk along the raised bank until a road bridge is reached.

6 Turn right and cross the bridge to soon pass an interesting little tollhouse. Just before a railway bridge, turn left on a signposted path that leads you back to the water's edge, where you continue rightwards. Remain alongside the river until you are opposite the village of Bury on the far bank.

7 At a marker post turn right and cross the centre of a field. More marker posts guide you towards Amberley. At one point you cross the railway so please take note of the signs. Soon pass the walls of the castle and remain ahead along the street until it ends at a T-junction. Turn left here to return to the Black Horse and the end of the walk.

Date walk completed:

....

Place of Interest
Amberley Working Museum is a 36-acre open-air museum, which preserves the industrial history of the south-east. It has plenty to interest all ages. Open Wednesday to Sunday from 10 am to 5 pm from end of March to the beginning of November (open daily during school holidays). Telephone: 01798 831370.

The Limeburners

A super walk that leads you over scenic fields where you discover a charming lake and also 'London's lost route to the sea' - the partially restored Wey & Arun Canal. After following the towpath for a short distance, the circuit turns northwards and crosses fields before passing through the appealing village of Wisborough Green.

Distance: *6¼ miles*

OS Explorer 134 Crawley and Horsham GR 073255

An easy walk on fairly level terrain

Starting point: The car park of the Limeburners but please seek permission from the landlord before leaving your car whilst you walk. Alternatively, park in the lane.

How to get there: The Limeburners is on the B2133, ½ mile west of the Billingshurst bypass (A29).

A quiet country lane then leads you to Newpound Common, where you rejoin the towpath of the canal.

The Limeburners, a 16th-century building, started life as a row of three lime-workers' cottages at New Bridge Wharf on the Wey & Arun Canal some ¼ mile away to the west. After the demise of the canal in the 1850s the building was transported to its present site and has been a popular pub ever since. Plenty of olde worlde charm invites you inside, where the food is good and the Gale's beers are superb. Watch out for the Horndean Special Bitter, which is deceptively strong!

Opening hours are 12 noon until 3 pm and 6 pm until 11 pm each day (Sunday 10.30 pm closing). Booking is advisable if you wish to eat a cooked meal.

Telephone: 01403 782311.

The Walk

1 With the Limeburners at your back, turn left along the road for a few yards before turning right along the driveway to Guildenhurst Manor. In 100 yards go left through a kissing gate and, shortly, through a second gate. Cross a large field diagonally rightwards on a distinct path. Exit the field via two gates and turn right along a well signposted footpath that skirts a paddock. Turn left immediately after crossing a small plank bridge over a stream and after 10 yards go right and cross a farm track. Continue ahead along the right-hand side of a field. Soon you will reach the bank of a pretty lake beside a small boathouse.

2 Turn right along the water's edge and at the end of the lake continue to the left to very soon cross a bridge. Now turn right along the bank of the River Arun. At the end of an open grassy area, cross a stile ahead of you and after 40 yards turn right onto a short uphill path that leads you through a bluebell wood. When you emerge at a field, turn immediately right and follow its edge to a field gate. Pass through the gate and ignore a farm track that forks to the right. The route continues ahead over a small-plank bridge after which you soon pass through a kissing gate. Now keep to the right-hand field edge and turn right through a further kissing gate to the bank of a restored section of the Wey & Arun Canal. Turn left here along the towpath and soon cross Lordings Bridge, rebuilt in 2002.

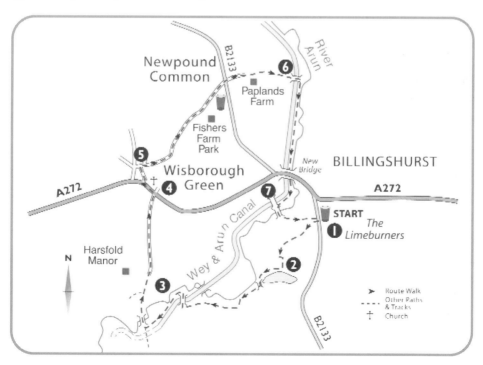

❸ Now continue left along the canal bank. Before long the restored canal ends abruptly. Cross a stile and maintain direction ahead until a further stile is met at a crossing track. Cross the stile and turn right along a wide track where you soon go over the River Arun. Pass through two field gates and follow a farm track over a field, later ignoring a path going left. When the track turns right into a farmyard, continue ahead on a narrow path through a gate and pass to the left of an old barn to soon join a driveway. Keep to this drive until you meet the A272 in Wisborough Green.

❹ Cross the road and enter Glebe Way. After 30 yards fork left onto a tarmac path that leads you to the church of St Peter Ad Vincula. Enter the churchyard and follow a narrow path that takes you to the far side of the church. Now go left on a flagstone path and exit the churchyard to emerge on a small residential road. Turn right to a small road junction.

❺ Turn right at this junction and soon pass the village school. Follow the country lane as it winds its way between fields and passes the occasional house. After Fisher's Farm Park and the highly recommended Bat and Ball public house, the lane ends at a road junction in Newpound Common. Here continue ahead on a bridleway that follows a farm drive. When the drive forks right into the farmyard, maintain direction ahead along the grassy bridleway. Pass through a field gate and continue along the left-hand field edge to soon rejoin the Wey & Arun canal.

❻ Cross a bridge and turn right along the towpath. During the summer months many dragonflies and damselflies are to be seen here and you may even be lucky enough to spot the occasional kingfisher. Follow this pretty path until it finally ends at a road. Cross the road to the path opposite and press on along the water's edge. Here you pass New Bridge wharf, once a hive of activity with large coal and timber yards lining the quay.

❼ Turn left at a junction of paths by a bridge over the canal and, with your back to the canal, follow a signposted path over a bridge that crosses the River Arun. The path goes uphill and crosses three fields to reach the driveway to Guildenhurst Manor. Turn left along the drive to reach a road where, by going left for a few yards, the pub is situated just to the left.

Place of Interest

Fisher's Farm Park is open from 10 am to 5 pm every day of the year except Christmas and Boxing Days. Sited 1½ miles north-west of the Limeburners and well signposted, there is plenty here for all the family to enjoy. Telephone: 01403 700063.

Date walk completed:

....

For the most part, this fairly level walk is along quiet lanes, private drives and scenic tracks. Starting off along the drive of Lock Farm, it crosses a branch of the River Adur that meanders through the fields here. Soon the route heads south, where the panoramic views across fields to the South Downs are extensive. More scenic views follow as the circuit meets another farm lane to reach the Downs Link long distance path.

The Partridge serves lashings of good food and fine ales. I like the motto printed on the front of the menu: 'There are no strangers here, just friends waiting to meet.' The wide selection of food on the menu includes dishes for the younger ones. The well stocked bar supplies a wealth of good beers and reasonably priced wines. There is a pleasant garden for summer days.

Distance: *6¾ miles*

OS Explorer 122 South Downs Way - Steyning to Newhaven
GR 189191

An easy walk on fairly level ground

Starting point: The Partridge pub. Park in the pub car park (please ask first) or around the village.

How to get there: Partridge Green is on the B2135 and is 3 miles north-west of Henfield. The pub is at the junction with the B2116.

Opening times are 11 am to 3 pm and 5 pm to 11 pm on weekdays and all day at weekends. Food is served during lunchtime and evenings with booking essential for cooked meals.

Telephone: 01403 710391.

The Walk

1 With the pub at your back, cross the B2135 and turn leftwards along it. The road soon goes over what was once a railway bridge and you should ignore a Downs Link path on your right but after 80 yards turn right along the private drive of Lock Farm. Follow this pleasant drive with far-reaching views to finally meet and cross the River Adur.

2 After crossing the river ignore a footpath to your right and remain on the drive. Soon, as the drive forks, continue ahead along a fenced bridleway that skirts a large garden. Ignore a footpath to your right at a gravel drive and keep ahead on the fenced bridleway. Soon pass to the left of modern barns, at the end of

which bear right at a fork. After passing close by a house, a T-junction is met where your way lies to the left on a bridleway along a farm track. The route now leaves this group of fine houses behind as the bridleway leads you between fields. Ignore a path to your right and remain ahead on the bridleway at all times.

3 Soon cross a small stream and continue along the fenced bridleway ignoring any footpaths to left and right. The bridleway zig-zags between fields and finally, after going down a gentle slope, meets a T-junction. Turn left to pass through a farmyard and meet a quiet lane. Turn right along the lane and continue along it until a road junction is met by Fox Cottage. Turn left here along

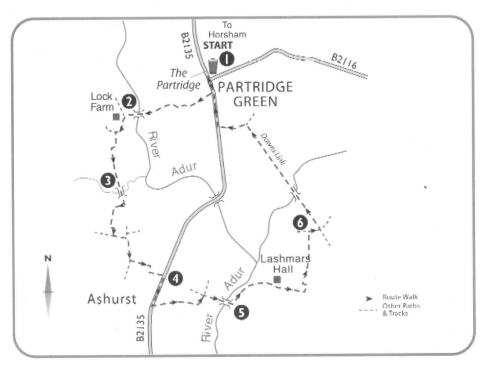

Golden Lane to finally arrive at the B2135.

4 Turn right alongside the road and continue to the outskirts of Ashurst. Turn left along a farm drive just before a house to your left. As you approach farm buildings, go left over a stile between a house and an outbuilding. At the end of a garden, turn right to cross a stile. Keep ahead over a field to another stile, which you cross to reach and cross a bridge over the Adur.

5 Turn left along the raised riverbank and continue until power cables cross the river at a bend by a stile. Here fork right over another stile and continue on a fenced path between two small ponds. Soon pass between a couple of fine old Sussex houses to reach a small driveway. Press on ahead now and remain on the drive until you pass a house on your right. After a further 50 yards, turn left along a farm track on a downward slope and continue along it until it divides.

6 The route is to the right along a signposted footpath that soon brings you to a large crossing track. This is the bed of the old railway and now forms a part of the Downs Link long distance path. Turn left along the path, where the only sound to break the quietness is the

Far reaching views along the route will be seen from the quiet lanes and farm tracks

birdsong that resounds from the hedgerows. This tranquil path has undergone something of a transformation since those days of steam when engines trundled along here with whistles blowing and sparks flying. Continue along this Downs Link path until it finally meets the B2135, where you now turn right alongside the road. Pass a few houses, two of which are quite ancient, to soon arrive back at the Partridge pub.

Date walk completed:

....

Place of Interest
Henfield Museum is in the village hall in Henfield's High Street. It illustrates the rural life of the area from medieval times by displaying domestic and agricultural objects as well as costumes, paintings and photographs. Open all year Monday, Tuesday, Thursday and Saturday from 10 am to 12 noon. Telephone: 01273 492546.

The Jack & Jill Inn

From the downland village of Clayton to the top of the rolling South Downs behind Brighton is where this lovely walk takes you. The path is steep but none too taxing if you have a rest or two along the way. At the summit the route passes Jack and Jill, two picturesquely sited windmills, and from the top of the downs there are spectacular views over wide open scenery.

The Jack & Jill Inn is a fairly modern and comfortable freehouse that has constantly changing real ales recognised by CAMRA and a wide choice of food including fresh local fish. The large garden is shared with ducks and geese, which children enjoy as much as they do the topsy-turvy playhouse.

Distance: *4 miles*

OS Explorer 122 South Downs Way - Steyning to Newhaven *GR 298143*

An easy walk with one steep hill

Starting point: The Jack & Jill Inn. Park in the pub car park (please ask first). Alternatively, start at the car park by the windmills (GR 304135).

How to get there: From the A23 at Pyecombe take the A273 towards Hassocks. The pub is ¾ mile on your left. For the alternative parking turn right up a lane signposted to the windmills before you reach the pub.

Opening times *are 11.30 am to 2.30 pm and 6 pm to 11 pm Monday to Friday, while on Saturday the hours are 11.30 am to 11 pm and on Sunday 12 noon to 11 pm. Food is cooked to order each day with last servings at 9.30 pm. Booking is necessary if wishing to consume a hearty meal here.*

Telephone: *01273 843595.*

The Walk

If you start the walk from the alternative parking by the windmills, read the instructions from point 2 first, leaving the point 1 instruction until last.

1 With the Jack & Jill Inn behind you, turn right along the busy road, which soon crosses a railway line just before it disappears into a fascinating tunnel entrance that incorporates a railworker's cottage. Press on past a road junction with the B2112 but within yards turn left into Underhill Lane. Pass the pretty church and look out for a bridleway on the right, beside Claytoncourt Stables. Follow this rising track to open downland. As the path becomes fainter, aim for the white painted windmill and

soon go right into a car park.

2 Go to the car park entrance and turn left along a stony track with the windmills to your left. After 150 yards ignore a marker post and remain ahead on the track. At a second marker post bear left along the well defined path and when you reach a gate across this track turn right onto a smaller fenced path just before it.

3 Soon, on a dip at a second gate, turn right onto a well-defined path along the field edge. With spectacular views over the countryside, and without further instruction, you should remain ahead on this downhill path until it finally passes the clubhouse of Pyecombe Golf Club and meets with a road.

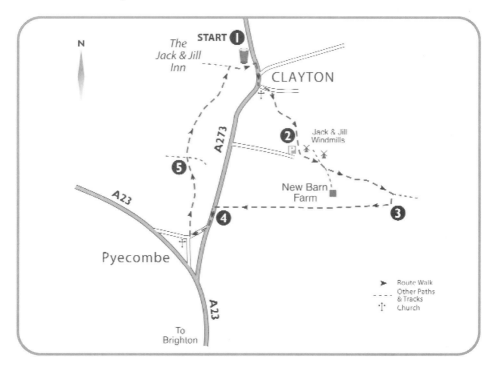

103

The Jack and Jill windmills from which the pub is named

4 Cross the road and go left along the footpath. Soon turn right into School Lane and before long turn right again into a road named The Wyshe. After passing houses and a small children's play area the route continues on an uphill bridleway.

5 At a junction of tracks alongside a Wolstonbury Hill National Trust sign you should maintain direction ahead. Ignore side paths as the bridleway now continues downhill through beech woodland and eventually ends at a small country lane. Turn right here and after passing a couple of cottages you are back at the Jack & Jill Inn and the end of this short excursion onto the South Downs.

> **Date walk completed:**
>
> ....

Place of Interest

Jill Windmill passed along the route has been restored to full working order. It is open to the public from May to September on Sundays and bank holidays from 2 pm until 5 pm. Telephone: 01273 843263

at Piltdown. It was near here, of course, that Charles Dawson carried out his famous Piltdown Man hoax back in 1912. As the circuit begins to make its way back towards Fletching, it passes through Grisling Common from where, as you walk through fields, you will enjoy far-reaching views across the Ouse valley and, directly ahead, the steeple of Fletching's 12th-century church will be seen. Finally the village road takes you through the churchyard before arriving at the Griffin Inn, where the walk ends.

S tarting off over open fields with extensive views of the surrounding countryside, this splendid walk takes you south and east of Fletching. After reaching the tiny hamlet of Down Street the route turns south and continues along a quiet country lane for a while before it heads off over the heath and golf course

The Griffin Inn is a lovely 16th-century inn still offering comfortable rooms for those passing this way. The owners are very proud of the two-acre garden, which they claim has some of the best views in Sussex. A wide choice of beer is offered as well as a plentiful supply of great food - not pub grub this, but fresh food produced by six chefs to an ever-changing menu.

Opening hours are 12 noon to 3 pm and 6 pm to 11 pm each day (Sunday 12 noon to 10.30 pm). Cooked food from 12 noon to 3 pm and 7 pm to 9 pm each day. Booking not required for bar food but essential for the restaurant.

Telephone: 01825 722890.

Distance: *5¼ miles*

OS Explorer 122 South Downs Way - Steyning to Newhaven GR 429235

An easy walk over undulating terrain

Starting point: The Griffin Inn. Park there (ask permission first) or in the free car park in the lane opposite.

How to get there: Turn northwards off the A272 in Piltdown to reach Fletching after 1 mile.

105

The Walk

1 Leave the Griffin Inn, turn right and then go left through a gate beside a cottage and enter the churchyard. Walk the length of the churchyard and towards the end fork left to a kissing gate. Ignore a path to the right and continue ahead diagonally across a field to cross a stile in the corner. Keep ahead to another stile and continue along a broad track to a field gate and cross a stile beside it. Go diagonally right over another field to cross a stile in a ribbon of woodland.

2 Cross a stream in a gully and continue over a stile. Go straight ahead over a field, and over the brow of the hill to a stile to the left of an oak tree. Cross this and bear right to cross a small bridge over a stream. Go ahead now through a gate beside a barn and out onto a quiet country lane.

3 Turn right along the lane to a T-junction in the hamlet of Down Street. Turn right here and continue for ¾ mile to turn right by a low concrete footpath sign pointing along a small driveway. Within yards, turn left and pass a barrier. Follow the path, which runs roughly parallel with the road, through heathland, with fields to your right. Continue ahead when a farm track crosses the path and soon pass farm buildings on your right to meet a driveway.

4 Cross a stile in the fence ahead and continue over the drive of Oak Ferrars Farm and through a gate. Continue ahead

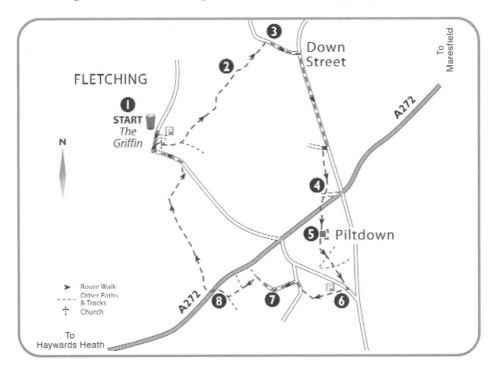

to a stile by an ornamental pond. Finally cross a further stile in the fence ahead before turning left to a road. Turn right for 30 yards then left onto a signposted footpath that soon leads to a driveway. Press on and soon cross a golf fairway. As you near a house follow a signposted path to the left that skirts the house and garden and pass to the right of the 16th tee.

5 Follow the path through a woodland and across a stream. Continue with the golf course on either side. As you meet the manicured grass, press on ahead between two greens. Bear left and pass behind the 4th tee then bear right to pass behind a green. Ignore a footpath to your right that leads to a road, and press on ahead on a path parallel to the road. By the 12th tee turn right to a road.

6 Cross the road and go along the left of a parking area to rejoin the golf course. Ignore the fairway that bears off to the right and continue ahead along the right-hand edge of the left fairway. At the end, continue past the 8th tee to meet a tarmac drive where you turn right to soon reach a road. Turn right along the road and after a bend turn left onto a lane signposted to Barkham Manor Vineyard.

7 When the gates of Barkham Manor are reached, fork right and soon the lane ends beside Cedar Lodge. Maintain direction along a path between banks and soon cross a stile in the hedge on your left. Now go ahead along the right-hand field edge to the end of the field. Cross a small wooden bridge and go rightwards over a stile. Now follow the edge of a field to arrive at a road.

8 Cross the road diagonally leftwards and turn right along the second of two driveways. The track passes between two houses and farm buildings to a farm gate. Cross a stile to the left of this into a large field. Go directly ahead down the dip towards the distant church spire. After crossing a stream, maintain direction over the next field to a farm track by power cables. Turn right and cross a stile beside a gate ahead. Go diagonally left to cross another stile and press on ahead along the right side of the recreation ground to a road. Turn left and soon right into the churchyard. Exit via the gate you passed through earlier and turn right to find the superb Griffin Inn.

Date walk completed:

....

Place of Interest
Sheffield Park Garden is a magnificent landscaped garden laid out by 'Capability' Brown in the 18th century. It is well signposted and lies 1 mile west of Fletching off the A275. Open early January to end of February at weekends from 10.30 am to 4 pm; March to end of October daily (except Mondays) 10.30 am to 6 pm, and November to December daily (except Mondays) 10.30 am to 4 pm. Telephone: 01825 790655.

The Anchor Inn

Some of the finest countryside in the south-east provides the setting for this unmissable walk. Rolling hills, distant views and pretty woodland all combine to make this a great excursion. Hartfield is just on the northern edge of Ashdown Forest and is where A. A. Milne lived and wrote his stories of Winnie the Pooh. Starting off by following the High Weald Landscape Trail across fields, the route meets up with the Weald Way, which it follows for some time. After walking through peaceful woodland the way meets with Chuck Hatch and from here it is just a short walk down into a valley where, in woodland, Pooh Bridge is crossed. Continuing through the valley the way reaches the oddly named hamlet of Gallypot Street. A quiet country lane and a wonderful farm track follow and lead you into the next valley and the Sussex Border Path. Turning eastwards along it the circuit eventually rejoins the High Weald Trail, which brings you back to the centre of Hartfield to complete the walk.

The Anchor Inn has its origins back in the 14th century. Occupying a picturesque spot in a street of old cottages, this lovely welcoming pub warrants a visit. The food is good and wholesome and includes sandwiches, baked potatoes, fish dishes and grills. From the pumps come Bass, Harvey's, Adnams and London Pride bitters plus Flowers IPA.

Opening times are from 11 am to 11 pm each day (Sunday 12 noon to 10.30 pm). Cooked food is available each lunchtime and evening. Booking is essential

Telephone: 01892 770424.

Distance: *7 miles*

OS Explorer 136 The Weald, Royal Tunbridge Wells
GR 479357

A moderate walk on undulating terrain

Starting point: The Anchor Inn. Park in the pub car park (with permission) or around the village.

How to get there: Hartfield is on the B2110 and 4 miles east of Forest Row. The Anchor Inn is in the centre of the village in Church Street.

The Walk

1 With the Anchor Inn at your back turn left and continue along Church Street. When opposite the church, turn right over a stile and then follow the waymarked High Weald Trail left through two fields. When entering a third field, ignore a path forking left and press on ahead over the centre of the field. Cross a stile in the bottom corner and continue ahead. Pass by the side of a house and stables and on along the left-hand edge of the field to meet a bridge over a stream.

2 Cross the bridge and immediately turn left on a waymarked path. Bear right at a fork after 50 yards and continue through woodland to reach a field, which you cross diagonally rightwards to the top corner. Turn right along a quiet lane that

forms a part of the Weald Way. It offers easy walking for a mile and has marvellous views over the undulating landscape. Finally the lane ends at a gateway to a large house.

3 Follow the signs leftwards on a narrow path that skirts the property and soon rejoins the lane at a junction of drives. Press on ahead and right along a drive signed as the Weald Way and pass a cottage named Forest Place. Here, at a fork in the drive, keep to the right. Follow the tarmac surface as it winds its way through peaceful woodland until it finally ends at a gate to a house. Continue ahead on a slowly rising stony cart track. At the top of a rise by a junction of paths leave the Weald Way by going ahead through trees to soon cross a footbridge over a woodland stream. In 30 yards ignore a left fork and continue ahead on a rising

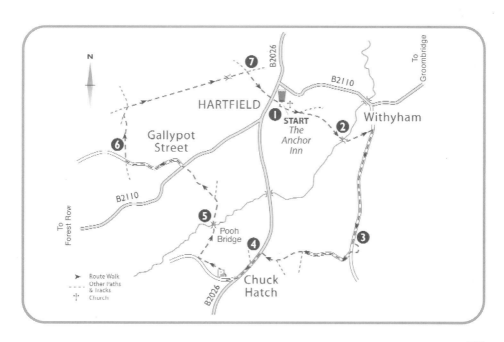

path that goes between banks and arrives at a road.

4 Go leftwards along the road and then turn right at a junction onto a lane signposted to Newbridge. After 200 yards bear right through Pooh car park and follow a path signed to Pooh Bridge. The well-trodden path brings you out to a lane by the gates of Andbell House. Go ahead for 60 yards and then turn right onto a bridleway signposted to Pooh Bridge. The path now leads you down into a valley, where you cross the famous bridge. It is not the 1907 original, which was repaired in 1979, but a new bridge in its image that had to be erected owing to the wear and tear caused by the thousands of feet that have trodden this way.

5 Cross Pooh Bridge and carry on ahead up the other side of the valley. Keep ahead on a private road and soon ignore a right fork; also ignore a footpath to your right by a house named Mole End and follow the road until it meets a junction in Gallypot Street. Press on ahead along Parrock Lane. Soon after it bends leftwards it becomes more rural and goes downhill to pass the entrance to Wayward Hill Farm. From here it begins to climb and 120 yards after going over the crest of the hill you turn right on a footpath along a stony farm track.

Pooh Bridge

6 The track offers fine rural views and brings you down into another valley. At a T-junction with another farm track turn right and after 100 yards meet a junction of paths by a gate. Here turn right along a level path that follows the bed of a disused railway. The Sussex Border Path and a section of a Regional Cycle Network share this path so watch out for the occasional cyclist.

7 About 250 yards after crossing a bridge a directional post is met. Here turn right along the signposted High Weald Trail and after crossing a couple of fields and the village recreation ground, the route returns to the Anchor Inn and the end of this enjoyable walk.

Date walk completed:

....

Place of Interest
For Pooh fans this is a must! **Pooh Corner** is a shop at the southern end of the village that contains all sorts of Pooh-phernalia. Once the village shop visited by Christopher Robin, it now specialises in anything to do with Winnie-the-Pooh. Open Monday to Saturday from 9 am to 5 pm and 1.30 pm to 5 pm on Sundays and Bank Holidays. Telephone: 01892 770872.

The Blackboys Inn

that leads to Hawkhurst Common. Here, you meet the Weald Way to cross more picturesque fields to reach the magnificent landscaped parkland of private Newplace Farm. Small ornamental cascades and waterfalls can be seen from the driveway as can the impressive house itself. Leaving the buildings behind, the circuit now continues through parkland before crossing more fields on the way back to Blackboys.

This fine walk takes you over open fields, with some great views across the surrounding countryside. The circuit follows parts of two long distance paths, the first of which is a scenic section of the Vanguard Way

Distance: *6 miles*

OS Explorer 124 Hastings & Bexhill
GR 522203

An easy walk on undulating terrain

Starting point: The Blackboys Inn, Blackboys. You can park along the verge in School Lane or in the pub car park, with permission.

How to get there: Blackboys is 4 miles east of Uckfield on the B2102. The pub is at the junction of the B2192 and School Lane (see map).

The Blackboys Inn is a Grade II listed building. It dates back to 1389 although it disguises its age very well. The cosy beamed interior is divided into three bars: public, saloon and snug, which makes a pleasant change from the large one bar pubs that are today's vogue. The beers are from Harvey's of Lewes and include their Sussex Best Bitter, IPA and Armada Ale. During the summer months you may choose to sit at a table in the pretty garden or under the covered pergola where a grapevine displays itself admirably.

Opening hours are from 11 am to 3 pm and 5 pm to 11 pm on Monday to Friday; 11 am to 3 pm and 6 pm to 11 pm on Saturday; and 12 noon to 3 pm and 7 pm to 10.30 pm on Sunday. For a table in the restaurant, it is advisable to book.

Telephone: 01825 890283.

111

The Walk

1 With the pub at your back, cross the B2192 and go through a field gate opposite to follow a distinct path down the centre of a field. Pass through a second gate and bear left alongside a hedgerow. Continue through another field gate and remain ahead until you meet a gate on your left. Do not go through it, but bear right downhill over the field to meet and cross two stiles and a bridge over a stream. Carry on over the next field and aim for a clump of pine trees where you pass through the left of two gates. Now go diagonally left across the centre of this rising field and pass through a gate in the top left corner. Maintain direction through a small coppice and a paddock and pass through a gate to the right of a house to soon meet a road.

2 Turn right along the road and, after 70 yards, bear right on a drive that is signposted as a private access road. Follow this drive until it finally ends in a farmyard. Pass between buildings and maintain direction ahead on a wonderful bridleway that leads you through woodland that is alive with birdsong. The bridleway ends at a lane where you turn right. When the lane bends sharply right, turn left on wide path, signposted Vanguard Way. Follow this lovely path until it ends at another country lane.

3 Go left and follow the lane to a T-

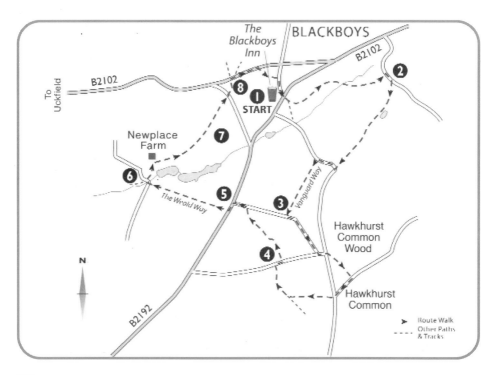

112

junction. Turn left here to very soon meet another T-junction. Go ahead and enter a field. Bear diagonally right to meet a marker post at a corner of Hawkhurst Common Wood. Bear right alongside the woodland to meet and cross a stile to come out at a lane. Turn right to soon meet a road junction. Here go diagonally right to meet a path that runs along the left side of a field. Cross a stile under an oak tree at the far side where you should maintain direction ahead to meet and cross another stile in the right-hand side. Here you meet the Weald Way long distance path. Go through a gully and cross a brook to reach another field. Walk ahead to a stile in the top left corner.

4 Cross a small lane and enter another field to reach a stile at the far side. Cross the stile and continue through another gully to reach another field. Go to the top left corner of the field and cross a stile. Press on ahead and cross a second stile by a bungalow to reach a lane. Turn left to very soon meet a T-junction.

5 Turn left along the road and after 80 yards turn right on a signposted Weald Way path that leads you directly over a field to meet a marker post by a corner of woodland. Keep ahead, with the woodland to your left. Maintain direction when the woodland ends and, after passing another marker post, you finally reach a quiet lane.

6 Still following the Weald Way, turn right and, within yards, right again along the drive to Newplace Farm. Follow the drive when it bends rightwards by low buildings and when it bends left towards a large barn, keep ahead along a well-defined cart track that passes through

lovely parkland. At a fork keep left and at a second fork bear left again as directed by the Weald Way signpost.

7 Cross a stile and head along the right-hand side of a rising field. Maintain direction to finally cross a stile by a gate in the top right corner of the field to a lane. Turn left along the lane for a short distance and then turn right by a cottage on a signposted path. Within yards, cross a stile and go left to follow the left side of a field to another stile in the corner to reach a road.

8 Turn right along the road and it is here that you finally leave the Weald Way. Some 80 yards after passing Tickerage Lane, turn right through a gate to reach Blackboys recreation ground. Go ahead and pass through a gate to the left of a children's play area to meet School Lane. Turn right back to Blackboys Inn which is just 300 yards along the lane.

Place of Interest
Bentley Wildfowl & Motor Museum is situated 4 miles west of Blackboys off the B2192. There is a fascinating collection of over 1,000 swans, geese and ducks plus a collection of veteran and vintage cars and motorcycles. It is open from 10.30 am to 5 pm daily from mid March to the end of October. Telephone: 01825 840573.

Date walk completed:

....

The Tiger Inn

The village of East Dean, which is the starting point of this superb walk, nestles snugly in a hollow less than a mile from the coast. Neat flint houses adorned with roses, magnificent village hall, cosy pub and picturesque green all go to make this an idyllic scene.

Distance: *6¾ miles*

OS Explorer 123 South Downs Way - Newhaven to Eastbourne
GR 557978

A challenging walk over hilly terrain

Starting point: The Tiger Inn. Park in the free car park 40 yards to the east (signposted from the A259).

How to get there: East Dean lies halfway between Eastbourne and Seaford on the A259.

The route heads for the Seven Sisters Country Park and the path traverses four of the seven clifftops known as the Seven Sisters before descending to reach Cuckmere Haven. Near the end of the circuit, lovely parkland is crossed by Friston.

The Tiger Inn is a pub with low beams, a cosy snug area by an open fire, a well stocked bar and a warm welcome. A good choice of snacks and homemade meals are served in ample portions, some with local freshly caught seafood. Outside are tables on a popular sunny patio that faces the village green.

Opening times are from 11 am to 3 pm and 6 pm to 11 pm Monday to Friday, 11 am until 11 pm on Saturday and from 12 noon until 10.30 pm on Sunday.

Telephone: 01323 423209.

The Walk

1 With the Tiger Inn behind you, cross the green to the left of the memorial to soon meet a small lane. Go left here and follow Went Way until it ends at a field gate. Continue through the gate and press on ahead up a steepish path to enter a ribbon of woodland. Maintain direction and, as you leave the trees behind, pass 50 yards to the right of a lonely barn. Here the way joins with a grassy farm track and you should press on ahead along it. Soon the track descends and continues through two field gates to arrive at Seven Sisters Cottage.

2 Continue for 20 yards past the cottage then turn right through a gate marked 'South Downs Way'. Follow this open path as it remains parallel to the cliff edge. There are notices suggesting that if you walk with a dog you should keep it on a lead for its own safety - good advice that should be followed. The path is close to the edge and sharply undulating, scenic and exhilarating.

3 After climbing the final rise, a fingerpost is met at which you bear right along the South Downs Way path. Ignore a stile to your left and remain ahead along the field edge with superb views of the River Cuckmere below you. At the end of this pleasant downhill path, the route meets a concrete farm track and your way is ahead along it until you come to the A259, which you should cross, with caution, to the Country Park museum and tearooms - an ideal place to stop off for refreshment.

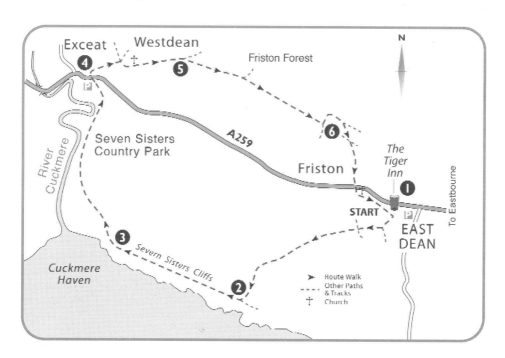

4 The route continues between a bike hire shop and a house to the right of the museum buildings, where you rejoin the South Downs Way. Cross a rising field to reach a couple of welcoming and well-placed seats. Cross a flint stile and press on ahead through woodland. Soon descend steep steps to reach Westdean by its little pond. Here you finally part company with the South Downs Way path as you turn right along a small lane that leads you past pretty houses, some being converted farm buildings. Carry on ahead up a rise to meet a fork in the road.

5 Keep to the right-hand fork and enter Friston Forest. When the road ends, keep ahead along the wide track through woodland. At a fork in the track by a post keep to the right and continue on the path now signed to Friston. Ignore side paths and keep ahead. At a downhill slope, just as the track bends to the left, carry on along a narrowing path. At a dip go over a crossing track and press on ahead on the path signposted to Friston. After passing open ground on your right the path descends and ends at a small lane.

6 Turn left along the lane and keep to it as it turns to the right. After 200 yards or so look out for a hidden gate in the flint wall on your right. Go through this and

The magnificent view westwards along the Seven Sisters cliffs

cross a field to a kissing gate at the far side. Press on over a stile ahead of you and continue through the next field to the top corner. Cross a stile and continue along an enclosed path to soon reach the A259. Cross with caution and enter the churchyard of Friston church via a unique gate. Pass to the right of the church and keep ahead to an open field. Now continue on a downhill path through a field to reach East Dean, the Tiger Inn and the end of this exhilarating walk.

Date walk completed:

....

The Merrie Harriers

This cracking walk crosses scenic fields soon after leaving the pretty hamlet of Cowbeech. The route then follows a small woodland stream that cuts deeply through a delightful wooded valley. As the way heads towards the tiny hamlet of Foul Mile, it crosses more splendid fields that offer peaceful and far-reaching views.

Distance: *4½ miles*

OS Explorer 123 South Downs Way, Newhaven to Eastbourne
GR 619145

An easy walk over undulating terrain

Starting point: The Merrie Harriers. Please ask permission to park in the pub car park, or park along nearby verges.

How to get there: Cowbeech is 2 miles north of the A271 at Herstmonceaux.

The Merrie Harriers is a delightful family-owned and run traditional Sussex pub. The grade II listed building dates back to the early 17th century as the beamed ceilings and large inglenook fireplace testify. The fine selection of food will stave off any hunger pangs. As well as lighter dishes there are main courses such as pan fried fillet of sea bass served on a bed of roasted Mediterranean vegetables. From the pumps come Harvey's Best, W J King's Horsham Ales and Tetley's Smooth, plus lagers and stout. Booking a table is advisable.

Opening hours are 11.30 am to 3 pm and 6 pm to 11 pm Monday to Saturday. Sunday hours are 12 noon to 3 pm and 7 pm to 11 pm.

Telephone: 01323 833108.

The Walk

1 With the pub at your back, cross the road and continue along the small lane opposite. When the lane dips and bends sharply right beside a field gate, turn left through the gate and enter a field. Now go diagonally right through the field to meet and cross a stile in a hedgerow. Press on ahead to meet and cross another stile beside an oak tree. Maintain direction ahead over more stiles until you enter a field with a coppice on your left and a house over to your right. Go diagonally right through this field, and aim just to the left of the house. As you near the end of the field cross a stile to the left of a field gate and continue downhill to meet a further stile, which you cross to meet a lane.

2 Turn right along the lane for 12 yards and then bear left on a signposted footpath through a ribbon of woodland with a stream to your left. After 25 yards, fork left and continue on a path that remains parallel to the stream. During early summer you will detect the garlic scent of ransoms that grow here so profusely. Soon, cross a stile and ignore a path to your right and continue ahead alongside the stream. At another stile maintain direction through this pretty valley. Look out for, and cross, a wooden bridge to your left. Now continue ahead along the left side of a field and at its end continue ahead uphill between trees to meet a stile on your left beside a farm gate and a concrete drive. Cross the stile and follow the drive until 10 yards after passing over a brook, bear right through

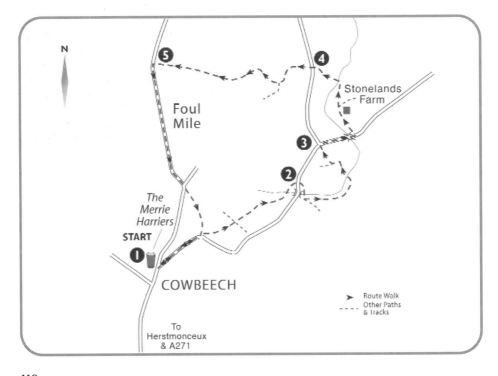

N

Foul
Mile

Stonelands
Farm

The
Merrie
Harriers

START

COWBEECH

To
Herstmonceux
& A271

➤ Route Walk
‑ ‑ ‑ Other Paths
& Tracks

a field gate. Ahead are three electricity pylons; our way is directly towards the middle one. Cross a stile in the far side and continue over a second to meet a quiet lane.

3 Turn right along the lane and when it dips go left along the drive to Stonelands Farm. Continue between the farmhouse and barns and cross a stile ahead of you. Now press on ahead and cross a stile in a dip ahead. The path continues through woodland with a small stream to your left. Look out for a directional post where you should turn left down steps and cross a two-plank bridge over the stream. Continue uphill and, at the top, turn left up steps and cross another bridge and stile. Go ahead along an all weather horse track to meet a field gate by a small pond. Turn left and cross a stile beside another gate ahead of you to meet a road.

4 Cross the road to a drive and continue along it until it ends by the gates of a house. Pass through the gates and bear right up a slope to a stile, which you cross to enter a field. Continue towards the centre of the rising field aiming towards a group of houses on the skyline. Over the crest of the hill, head towards a stile. Cross this and press on ahead through the next field to cross a wooden bridge. Go ahead along the right side of a field to its top corner. Enter another field and bear half right to a stile 10 yards to the right of a tree in the hedgerow ahead. Cross this and go diagonally half left to a gate that

is 20 yards to the left of a power cable post. Go through the gate and continue along the right-hand field edge to finally pass through another gate to meet a road.

5 Turn left along the road, passing the pretty cottages of Foul Mile, a name the hamlet does not deserve. After passing these cottages the road goes around an S-bend and, on the second of these, go left over a stile at a farm entrance. Continue ahead over a field and pass through a gate in the right-hand corner. Now turn right through a second field and through a gate to reach a lane. Turn right here and retrace your steps back to the Merrie Harriers at Cowbeech.

Place of Interest
Herstmonceaux Castle is a 15th-century moated castle set in 300 acres of tranquillity. There is a gift shop, visitor's centre, nature trail and children's play area. Open daily from April to October between 10 am and 6 pm (5 pm during winter). Special days include the Easter egg hunt, a classical open-air concert with fireworks and a medieval festival. Telephone: 01323 833816.

Date walk completed:

....

This superb walk begins on a ridge that runs between the Rother valley and the smaller Dudwell valley. After crossing scenic fields, the route descends into the Rother valley where the views are delightful. Leaving the valley behind, the way climbs easily back to the ridge, which is crossed by the hamlet of Burwash Weald. The circuit then descends through glorious fields and woodland to meet the clear waters of the River Dudwell and pass a restored watermill.

The Bell Inn is a lovely 16th-century pub set in the tree-lined main street. It hides its maturity well amongst other aged buildings in this conservation area. Step into the cool interior and sample the wide choice of good food from either the bar or à la carte menus. Children have their own choices. The range of beers is superb and includes Greene King IPA, Ruddles Best, Morlands Bitter and Old Speckled Hen, as well as Carlsberg, Kronenbourg, Scrumpy Jack and Guinness.

Opening hours are from 12 noon to 3.30 pm and 4.30 pm to 11 pm Monday to Friday, with all day opening at weekends. Food is cooked each lunchtime and evening, except Sunday evening. Booking is necessary if in a party of over six.

Telephone: 01435 882304.

Distance: *6½ miles*

OS Explorers 123 South Downs Way - Newhaven to Eastbourne and 124 Hastings & Bexhill
GR 677248

An easy walk, on undulating ground.

Starting point: The Bell Inn, Burwash. Park in the pub car park, with permission, or along the verges in the lane opposite the pub.

How to get there: Burwash is on the A265, 4½ miles west of the A21 at Hurst Green.

The Walk

1 With your back to the pub, cross the road and enter St Bartholomew's churchyard. Continue on a path to the right of the church and very soon keep ahead at a fork and enter a field. Keep ahead along the left edge and ignore a stile on your left. Pass through a kissing gate and ignore a path to your right. Keep ahead and ignore an inviting gate on your left at the end of the field. Carry on along a field edge, passing farm buildings. At the end of the field cross a stile by a gate and bear left along a short drive to meet a road.

2 Turn right along the road and 50 yards after passing tile hung cottages, turn left over a stile and keep to the right side of a downhill field. As the field ends, press ahead alongside trees to cross a small bridge over a stream. Now go ahead on a path to meet a lane and turn right. After 120 yards, turn left through a gate on a signposted bridleway. The bridleway passes through what looks like a garden where you pass between a pond and a bungalow to meet a farm track. Continue ahead through a field and pass between farm buildings to meet and cross a stile.

3 Go straight ahead through the centre of a field, following a line of power cables. At the far side, go through a field gate and cross a stream. Turn diagonally half left to meet and cross a bridge. Turn right along a field edge. In 80 yards, at the corner of the field, ignoring a path ahead, take the path left along the field edge following a waymarked bridleway. Keep a hedgerow to your right and when this ends, press on ahead to a marker post at the far end of the field. Maintain direction through a second field and aim

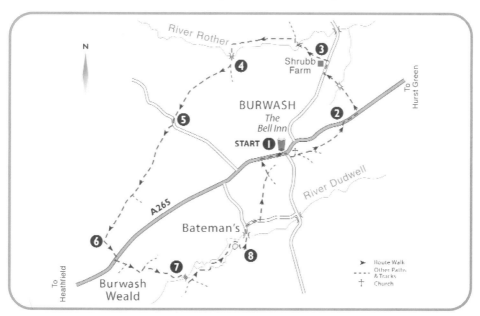

for a clump of trees ahead of you. When alongside these trees by another marker post, turn left and cross a bridge over the River Rother.

❹ Go ahead along the side of a field to meet its corner. Ignore a stile on your left and turn right along the rising field edge. Cross a stile and follow a rising track. When this bends right at a field, keep ahead and continue through a field gate and along a field edge. Turn right over a stile beside a gateway and then continue leftwards along the drive. Keep to the drive until it ends at a lane.

❺ Turn left along the lane and in 40 yards turn right on a bridleway beside a fine old farmhouse. For the next mile the way continues along this path until it finally ends at a farm track.

❻ Turn left along the farm track and soon fork left. Maintain direction at a driveway to meet a road. Turn right and, in 20 yards, go left on a public footpath along a drive. Go through a farm gate. Ignore a path forking right and keep ahead to a kissing gate in 40 yards. Pass through a field gate to reach a second kissing gate. Bear left to reach a gate where the path divides. Do not pass through this gate, but turn right and go downhill to reach woodland and on to the River Dudwell.

❼ Keep ahead and soon cross a bridge over the river. Ignoring a path to your right, turn left through a field and pass through the right-hand of two gates ahead of you. Turn left over a wooden bridge and pass through a field gate. Now turn right on an indistinct path through a field with a stream to your right. Continue through a kissing gate. Ignore a bridge on your left and keep to the main path where in 40 yards you should pass through a gate. Soon pass a newly restored millpond and the lovely old mill that was once owned by Rudyard Kipling.

❽ At Corner Cottage, go left along a drive and when opposite Bateman's, turn right along a quiet lane. Look out for, and cross, a stile on your left. Now press on ahead up a rising field and cross a stile. Continue forward and pass to the right of a small coppice to meet and go over the stile to reach and cross another stile and a small bridge. Continue ahead over another field and at the far side cross a stile by an oak tree. The path now divides and our route is left to finally cross a stile and meet a small car park. Go out to the road and turn right to the Bell Inn.

Place of Interest
Bateman's became the home of Rudyard Kipling in 1902 and after his death in 1936 his wife gave it to the National Trust. It is situated off the A265, ½ mile west of the Bell Inn. Open April to October from Saturday to Wednesday. Telephone: 01435 882302.

Date walk completed:
....

The White Dog Inn

E whurst Green, an elevated village that lies to the south of Bodiam Castle, is the starting point of this superb walk. The village is a delight and the circuit starts by passing fine houses that line the single street. Soon the route heads off over fields that offer marvellous views across the vale. As it nears the castle it meets the peaceful bank of the River Rother. After leaving the river, the circuit begins to head back to Ewhurst Green and climbs easily out of the valley crossing scenic fields.

The White Dog Inn is a delightful pub that has much to offer, with a wide choice of superb beers and food, but be careful of the variable opening hours.

Opening times are 6.30 pm to 11 pm on Monday, 11.30 am to 3 pm and 6.30 pm to 11 pm Tuesday to Friday, 11.30 am to 11 pm Saturday and 12 noon to 3 pm and 7 pm to 10.30 pm on Sunday. Food is cooked from 12 noon to 2 pm and 7 pm to 9 pm from Tuesday to Friday, 12 noon to 2 pm and 7 pm to 9 pm on Saturday and only from 12 noon to 2 pm on Sunday.

Telephone: 01580 830264.

Distance: *4¼ miles*

OS Explorer 124 Hastings & Bexhill GR 796246

A fairly easy walk

Starting point: The White Dog Inn. Park in the pub car park (please ask first) or along the village street.

How to get there: Follow signs from the A229 to Bodiam Castle. Pass this and then follow signs to Ewhurst Green.

The Walk

1 Leaving the front of the pub, turn right along the village street. Continue past picturesque houses until you meet a kissing gate on your right when opposite the rectory. Go through the gate and continue along the side of a large field. Pass through a second kissing gate in the bottom left corner and cross a stile after 10 yards. Now turn right to soon meet a second stile, which you cross, and maintain direction ahead along the field edge. Towards the end of this field bear left to cross a stile by a finger post.

2 Now turn rightwards to soon cross a stile and a two-plank bridge over a

stream. Keep ahead now with a ditch on your left and cross yet another stile and planked bridge alongside a barn. After passing the barn, go left and cross two stiles in quick succession to cross a railway line, with caution.

3 Now follow the field edge rightwards before turning left along its far border to soon reach the bank of the River Rother. Turn left along the bank and as you near a road, fork left to cross a stile. Turn right along the road and go over the road bridge. Ahead is the entrance to Bodiam Castle and its tearooms which make a pleasant place to stop for refreshment on a warm day. Our route continues leftwards immediately after crossing the

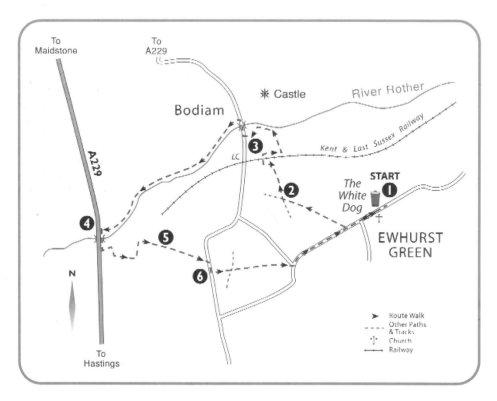

bridge. Now follow a path along the riverbank until you finally meet a road.

4 At the road, turn left over the road bridge and soon go left again along the driveway of Udiam Farm. After crossing a stream, go right over two stiles in quick succession to find a fingerpost. Now turn left along the rising field edge and pass stabling. At the top corner of the field go over a stile and turn right to meet a farm track. Go left along the track and 30 yards after passing a large brick building turn right through a field gate and continue along the left side of a rising field.

5 As you cross the crest of the hill bear slightly right to meet a marker post. Keep ahead now with a ditch to your immediate left and an orchard beyond it. Cross a stile in the bottom left corner of the field and maintain direction over another stile and a planked bridge. Remain ahead along the left field edge to cross another stile and small bridge. Press on ahead and cross a stile to meet a road.

6 Turn right along the road for 40 yards before crossing a stile on your left. Follow an indistinct path over a rise in the field to cross a stile at the far side. Here ignore paths to left and right and press on ahead through an organic orchard. At the end of the orchard, continue through pretty woodland to reach a small paddock. Keep ahead through the paddock to finally cross a stile beside a field gate.

'Preachers' is just one of the fine old houses the circuit passes

Now go ahead along the lane signposted to Ewhurst Green, where, before long you will find the White Dog Inn and the end of this lovely circuit.

Place of Interest

Bodiam Castle is a picturesque 14th-century fortification surrounded by a moat and set within beautiful parkland. Owned by the National Trust since 1926, it is open daily from mid February to October, from 10 am until 6 pm or dusk if earlier and from November to mid February at weekends from 10 am to 4 pm. Telephone: 01580 830436.

Date walk completed:

....

The Bridge Inn

A lovely path that follows the banks of the Royal Military Canal makes up the first section of this interesting figure of eight walk. The path takes in the last 2½ miles of this 28-mile long canal that stretches from Hythe in Kent to Cliff End at Pett Level. The canal ends rather ingloriously in a reed bed, just yards from the sea and it is here that the way changes direction and follows the seashore eastwards. To complete the figure of eight the way turns inland and passes under picturesque New Gate, once a part of Winchelsea's fortifications.

The Bridge Inn is a pretty pub that has a small bar with low beams and a village atmosphere, while the separate dining area is as comfortable as any you can find. From the pumps come Harvey's Bitter and Courage Best plus Stella Artois, Heineken, Murphy's stout and Strongbow cider.

Opening times are 11.30 am to 3 pm and 6 pm to 11 pm (Sundays 12 noon to 10.30 pm). Cooked food is served from 11.30 am to 2.30 pm and 6 pm until 9.30 pm (Sundays 12 noon until 9 pm). Booking is advisable at weekends.

Telephone: 01797 226453.

Distance: 5¾ miles

OS Explorer 125 Romney Marsh, Rye & Winchelsea
GR 908177

An easy walk on flat ground

Starting point: The Bridge Inn. Park in the pub car park (with permission) or in lay-bys either 200 yards along the A259 to the north of the pub or in nearby Sea Road.

How to get there: Winchelsea is 2 miles west of Rye. The pub is on the A259 by a sharp bend to the east of the town.

The Walk

1 With the Bridge Inn behind you, go left and cross the main road into Sea Road. After 50 yards go right over a stile opposite a bus stop. Here you follow the canal bank eastwards with the town of Winchelsea peering over the tree line to your right. Look out for the bird life as heron, curlew and lapwing, as well as the resident swans, can be seen here. Keep to the canal bank until it ends beside a cottage. Turn left along a concrete drive to soon meet the coast road.

2 Turn left along the road and continue for 50 yards, then climb steps to reach the sea wall. The route continues eastwards now along the sea wall. As you pass Pett Pools, a popular spot for 'twitchers', you may get a chance to see some rare water birds. About ¼ mile after passing these pools go left down steps by a marker post.

3 Cross a stile on the far side of the road and another by a gate diagonally to your right. Now continue leftwards beside a stream on a well-defined path. Keep to this path and head for white cottages in the distance at the foot of a low hill. Cross a small bridge over a stream to meet the canal bank. Go over a second bridge that crosses the canal and continue ahead along the left side of a rising field to meet a lane.

4 Turn right along the lane and soon pass under New Gate, a part of the fortified town wall. A few yards on you

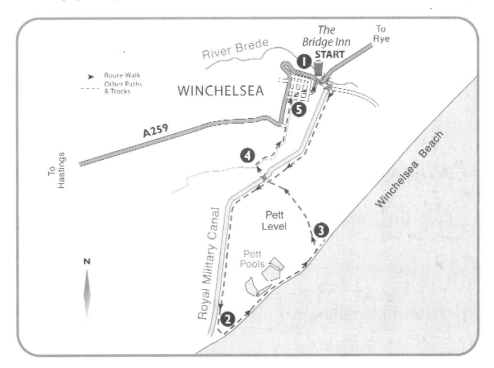

127

Looking eastwards along the beach at Pett Level during high tide

will see man-made mounds to your left that are topped by trees. This site is known as 'The Plague Pit' as it is said to contain the bodies of those taken by the Black Death in 1348. Press on along the lane, keep ahead at a road junction and enter Winchelsea proper.

5 Turn right through the gate of St Thomas's church and, after passing through an arch, fork right to meet Winchelsea's High Street. Press on rightwards along the road to arrive at Strand Gate, another fortified gateway and from which there are lovely views seaward. Continue under the arch as the road descends to meet the A259, where by turning right you reach the Bridge Inn and the end of this lovely walk.

Date walk completed:

....

Place of Interest

A walk around the old town of **Winchelsea** is interesting in itself. The streets are laid out in a grid system and are bordered by many pretty houses. In the High Street opposite St Thomas's church is the **Court Hall** a lovely building and one of the town's oldest. The ground floor once served as the town jail and is not open to the public but on the first floor there is an interesting museum displaying many local artefacts. Telephone: 01797 224395.